Cold War

in a

Cold Place

The snow-packed story
of the 511th AC&W Group
and the men who helped
preserve the peace
in a world on the brink
of destruction.

Compiled and Edited
by Jerry Hanks

Copyright © 2005 by Jerry Hanks

ISBN 0-7414-2707-9

Published by:

INFINITY
PUBLISHING.COM

1094 New De Haven Street, Suite 100
West Conshohocken, PA 19428-2713
Info@buybooksontheweb.com
www.buybooksontheweb.com
Toll-free (877) BUY BOOK
Local Phone (610) 941-9999
Fax (610) 941-9959

Printed in the United States of America

Printed on Recycled Paper

Published August 2005

Contents

Prologue and Acknowledgments

This book started in a banquet room at the 2000 reunion of the 511th AC&W Group in Arlington, Virginia. That's when Roger Wolf cornered me and said that he had heard I was a writer and editor and that he thought I should put together a book about the 511th Aircraft Control & Warning Group and its related squadrons, radar detachments and other units.

I may have had one beer too many and instead of saying no, I told Roger I'd sleep on it. That suited Roger. At the farewell breakfast the next morning, before we all headed home, Roger brought up the subject again.

Roger, if you don't know him personally, is a tough person to turn down, not because he's so aggressive or hard to handle but because he's so pleasant that you don't want to disappoint him. Roger was a Philco tech rep at Site 45 in 1954-55 and in more recent years played a leading role in compiling the roster of 511th personnel – decades after we all thought we had seen each other for the last time. Roger's task was enormous and his success was overwhelming – as one glance at the roster will prove.

So I told Roger yes and you're holding the result in your hands. Actually, what you're holding is the first of what is intended to be two results. A second edition of the book, containing pictures and additional chapters, is already in the works.

I can hardly begin to acknowledge everyone who has helped to make this first edition possible. Certainly at the top of the list are Roger and the 511th's executive secretary, Don Simmons, who have stuck with me through one prolonged personal illness, and the death of my father. Ranking alongside Roger and Don among those to be thanked are all of the 511th members whose stories make this book unique. Without their help – and their incredible anecdotes – there would be no book.

I'd also like to thank Pat Wise, a personal friend and a fellow member of the 511th from Site 28, for his untiring assistance in reviewing each chapter for technical accuracy; Jennifer Holland, for her work in designing the cover; Mike Rosenberg, for his computer genius, and my beloved wife Bobbi, a gifted writer and editor herself, for her untiring support as editor pro bono and publishing facilitator supreme. My special thanks also are extended to Michelle Shane and all of her co-workers at Infinity Publishing for preparing this book in its final form.

To all of you, and to any I may have overlooked, please accept my sincere appreciation.

Jerry Hanks
Jacksonville, Florida
2005

INTRODUCTION

Preserving the Peace
In a World
On the Brink of Destruction

The story was buried deep inside the daily newspaper in a roundup titled, "World Briefing." In its entirety, the story read:

2 RUSSIAN PLANES ENTER
JAPANESE AIRSPACE

TOKYO -- Two Russian planes illegally entered Japan's airspace yesterday. Tokyo issued a strong protest, a Japanese official said.

After a Russian Su-24 fighter was spotted on radar screens yesterday, four Japanese F-15 fighters scrambled toward the plane, but no encounter occurred, said Ichiro Imaizumi, a defense agency official. He said the Russian fighter violated Japan's airspace for one minute off Kyurokujima Island, 330 miles north of Tokyo.

Earlier, a Russian plane was spotted off Rebunto Island at the tip of Japan's northernmost main island of Hokkaido, the official said.

Because of bad weather, Japan warned the plane to leave its airspace by radio from the ground, Imaizumi said.

For those who were involved in the air defense of Northern Japan in the decade and a half after the end of World War II, the words in the story are likely to provoke little more than a yawn and the comment, "So, what else is new?" Except for one thing. . .

The date on the story, which appeared in *The Florida Times-Union* in Jacksonville, was April 12, 2001.

The years pass by. The players change. But the game goes on. You probe our defenses. We'll probe yours. Of course, not much is going to be said about the latter. At least not officially. But bit by bit the story trickles out (and if you want to read more see a book titled "By Any Means Necessary," written by William E. Burrows).

The last of the troops from the 613th and 848th AC&W Squadrons had been gone from the radar sites of Northern Honshu and Hokkaido for more than 40 years when the story appeared. The radar sites today are manned by the Japanese Self Defense Force. The pilots are Japanese and they fly F-15s instead of F-86s and F-100s, and they square off against SU-24s instead of MIGs.

But the game which started in 1945 continues today.

The "Cold War" is over now. At its peak it was "cold" only in comparison with the "hot war" which ended on August 10, 1945, when the Japanese notified the United States of its intention to surrender after atomic bombs had devastated the cities of Hiroshima and Nagasaki.

2

After the surrender, Japan lay defenseless and in ruins. Its economy was destroyed by the war which had started in 1931 with the Japanese invasion of Manchuria; escalated with the full scale invasion of China in 1937, and exploded into global conflict with the bombing of Pearl Harbor on December 7, 1941. By 1945 the Japanese populace faced mass starvation and the country's cities and industrial might were crushed by the incessant bombing in the latter stages of the war.

To add to the peril facing the defeated nation, the island chains to the north and northeast of the northernmost island of Hokkaido, which once belonged to Japan, now belonged to the Communists of the Soviet Union.

In February 1945, Stalin, Churchill and Roosevelt held a conference at Yalta in the Russian Crimea to map the strategy that would bring World War II to a close. The end of the war in Europe was in sight, with the Russians pounding the retreating German army in the east and Allied forces surging across Europe toward the German heartland from the west.

But Roosevelt and Churchill were far less confident about bringing the war against Japan to a speedy conclusion and Russia's help in the Far East was deemed a vital necessity. Stalin did not disagree but he had a price. Russia and Japan had been at odds since 1904 when Japan declared war on Russia and attacked the Russian fleet stationed in northern China.

Now Russia wanted more of a buffer to discourage any future Japanese encroachment in Siberia. Specifically, Stalin wanted control of the Kurile Islands, which stretched northeastward toward the tip of America's Aleutian Islands, and he wanted control of the southern portion of the Sakhalin Islands, due north of Hokkaido, to go along with the northern sector already controlled by Russia.

It must have sounded like a small price to Churchill and Roosevelt and the deal was struck. Stalin agreed to enter the war against Japan three months after the defeat of Germany. No mention was made of U.S. efforts to develop an atomic bomb. And no one could have predicted what was about to happen.

First, Roosevelt died on April 12, 1945 and was succeeded by Harry Truman. The war in Europe ended on May 8. Truman ordered the U.S. to drop its first atomic bomb on Hiroshima on August 6.

Two days later -- and exactly three months after the surrender of Germany -- Stalin kept his promise and declared war on Japan. The very next day the U.S. dropped its second atomic bomb on Nagasaki. And the day after that Japan notified the U.S. of its decision to surrender. So two days after entering the war against Japan, the Soviet Union gained control of the Sakhalin and Kurile Islands without ever firing a shot. And, much to the chagrin of the Japanese, that's the way it is today.

It didn't take long after the end of hostilities for the world to begin to separate into two armed camps: the capitalist West and the communist East. The split presaged the beginning of the Cold War which would go on for well over 30 years, numbing the world with the spectre of a nuclear holocaust and with peace based on the flimsy premise of "mutual armed destruction."

The capitalist West, and the United States in particular, needed a strong ally in the Far East to discourage communist aggression. So the decision was made to help the old ruling class in Japan reconstitute the government-business partnership which had built Japan into such a formidable power. General Douglas MacArthur, commander of the occupational forces, was placed in charge of restoring the old order, except for outright militarism.

While all of this was going on, the United States would defend Japan from an enemy which now occupied land within eyesight across the straits from the northern and eastern tips of Hokkaido. By 1946, the first steps were taken to implement an early warning system which would protect the skies of Northern Japan.

In the years which followed, crisis after crisis stretched the global tension between West and East.

As early as 1947, President Truman pledged U.S. support to fight communism throughout the world.

In 1948, the communists seized control of the governments in 12 eastern European countries.

In 1949, the Soviets detonated their first atomic bomb. In the same year, Mao Tse-tung declared China a communist republic and Germany officially was divided into East and West.

Then, on June 25, 1950, the military forces of North Korea (a land administered by the Soviet Union) attacked South Korea, a country administered by the United States. In short order, the Chinese communists entered the fighting on the side of North Korea.

Four bloody years later, just as peace was being restored in Korea, the communists led by Ho Chi Minh defeated the French at Dien Bien Phu. Vietnam, like Korea, was divided into two parts, setting the stage for the Viet Nam conflict which went on until the U. S. Embassy in Saigon closed its doors in the spring of 1975.

Through all of this global turmoil, the reconstruction of Japan stood out as an amazing story of success. And although its American maintained and operated defenses were often probed they were never breached.

For that a large amount of credit belongs to those who helped to scan the skies of Northern Japan for the better part of 15 years and kept the cold war cold -- in more ways than one.

Bibliography

Vadney, T. E. *The World Since 1945.*
   London: Penguin Books. Third Edition. 1998.

Courtenay-Thompson, Fiona and Kate Phelps.
   The 20th Century Year by Year.
   New York: Barnes & Noble Books. 1998.

1

GENESIS

The 613th AC&W Squadron
And How It All Began

In the beginning, the Army created the 613th Aircraft Control & Warning Squadron. There was no Air Force and, somewhat like the biblical account of the creation of the universe itself, the squadron was without form and void.

Many weeks later the first order was cut assigning an officer to the newly formed squadron. His name was Robert E. Linder. The date of the order was August 1, 1946, and for 15 years there followed after him hundreds and then thousands of others, dispatched to places with strange sounding names like Funagawa and Abashiri and Erimo-Zaki and Okushiri-Shima.

Many were barely out of high school and still in their teens. Some were battle-decorated veterans of the global conflict which had ended just 11 months earlier in the atomic desolation of Hiroshima and Nagasaki. Some were radar operators and radar mechanics. Some were truck drivers and supply sergeants. Some were cooks and some were clerks. Some were commanders of radar sites and entire squadrons. They came because they were ordered to come and they did their job to the best of their energies and skills, defending the skies of Northern Japan against an enemy they never saw and defying the storms of winter that sometimes staggered the imagination.

They were the men of the 613th AC&W Squadron, and later the 847th and 848th AC&W Squadrons and the 511th AC&W Group, and all of the radar detachments that dotted the perimeter of Northern Honshu and the northern island of Hokkaido.

Together they formed the first line of detection and defense against any encroachment of the air space over Northern Japan in the tension-filled years of the late 1940s and the Korean War which followed.

Slowly, day after day, month after month, each of the men who came to Japan counted the time off the calendar until they could go back to their homes in the states or be sent to another assignment, hopefully in a more habitable part of the world.

After they had left, often many years later, they would come to realize that although it was easy to leave the snow and the cold and the long gray months of winter, it was altogether impossible to remove from their minds the kinship they shared with the others they knew at places like Nemuro and Ominato and Wakkanai.

In its early years, the 613th AC&W Squadron was located at Johnson Field (later Johnson Air Base), near Tokyo. Eight days after 1st Lt. Linder was assigned as the squadron's first officer, Sergeant Raymond E. Blenkinsop, a radar mechanic, was assigned as the first enlisted man.

The squadron grew quickly. By the end of September, there were 163 enlisted personnel. Most were basic soldiers (the Air Force was not created until September 18, 1947), who were to be trained for highly specialized jobs especially in the use of radio and radar equipment. Others were experienced housekeeping personnel chosen to help in setting up an orderly room and converting the former base school building into a combination barracks and head-quarters.

Lt. Linder's command did not last long. On September 11 he became the squadron's communications officer and Major Richard P. Ozier Jr. assumed command of the squadron.

Japan was virtually defenseless at the time and things moved quickly. In October, the squadron turned its attention to establishing the first radar station at Hyoga-Zaki, on the northernmost tip of Hokkaido. The location was to be known as Site 17.

First Lt. Tony J. Oliveto directed the acquisition of the technical equipment and personnel for the new site. Within a month the site was operational and lst Lt. Lamar C. Noble became officer-in-charge while Lt. Oliveto turned his attention to organizing additional sites, including Site 4 at Chitose Army Air Base on Hokkaido.

It didn't take long for the Site 17 team to experience its first action. On Nov. 17, 1946, radar operators picked up unidentified surface craft on their scopes. Planes were dispatched but were late in arriving because of communication difficulties. By the time they got to the scene, the bogies were gone. But the presence of surface craft was confirmed by men in the CIC detachment at nearby Wakkanai, who spotted the craft with binoculars.

High winds also caused excitement, damaging the antenna and curtailing operations until repairs were made. The solution was to build a screen to enclose the entire set and protect it from the wind.

Meanwhile the team at Site 4 at Chitose was designated as the NET Control Station for the reporting net and necessary radio equipment was installed. A direct phone connection was also installed to 49th Fighter Group Operations at Chitose. The bad news at Chitose was that the radar required considerable overhauling and was still inoperative.

Survey crews also were scouting Hokkaido for additional radar sites. Several desired locations were ruled out because of their inaccessibility in bad weather but a site at Rumoi on the northwest coast showed promise.

By January 1947 the radar at Chitose was operational and by February Site 14 at Rumoi had joined the network and Site 13 at Esashi on the southwest coast of the island was under consideration.

By the end of 1947, the 613th squadron headquarters was relocated to Misawa Air Base on northern Honshu and its operations were placed under the control of the 528th AC&W Group, which remained at Johnson. The 528th was also responsible for similar operations in central and southern Japan.

In 1948 the site numbers were changed. Site 17 became Site 18 at Wakkanai. Site 13 at Esashi became Site 16, and Site 14 at Rumoi became Site 30. By 1949, Site 2 at

Misawa and a new Site 14 at Funagawa on the west side of northern Honshu became operational.

Over the next two years, the network was further expanded with the addition of Site 34 at Shiriya Saki on northeastern Honshu, and Site 32 at Matsumae and Site 36 at Erimo-Zaki, both on southern extremities of Hokkaido. The perimeter defense of northern Japan was now in place although there would be many changes and improvements in the decade of the 1950s.

2

THE FLIGHT
THAT NEVER MADE IT

Eddie Eugene (Gene) Walker
Radar Operator, Site 42, Ominato
613th AC&W Squadron

Of all the guys who manned the radar sites in Northern Japan, I'm sure I'm one of the few who had ever lived in Japan before being sent there by the Air Force.

I was an Army brat, born at Fort McClellan Army Hospital in Anniston, Alabama. I lived in Japan when I was 8 to 12 years old while my father was stationed at Osaka. But the experience didn't help much when I was sent to Site 42 at Ominato in 1957. In fact, I almost didn't make it to Japan at all.

When I was in basic training at Lackland I became buddies with Jim Johnson. We went to radar school at Keesler together and then we were both assigned to Japan. When we got to Travis Air Force Base in California there were so many troops ahead of us that we had to wait several days for a MATS flight. When our time finally came, I called my parents and then we went to the air terminal.

Just as we were to board the C-97, someone noticed that our duffel bags weren't stenciled properly. Believe it or not, we were bumped until the stenciling met Air Force regulations.

A few hours later another flight was leaving and we boarded that one. On the Honolulu to Wake Island leg of the flight, it seemed that we were flying awfully low -- so low, in fact, that you could see the white caps on the waves. But we made it to Wake without any trouble and then, after refueling, we flew on to Tokyo at what seemed to be a normal altitude.

When we landed I was met at the plane and told to call home immediately. My heart sank. When I reached my parents I found that they had heard on the news that the flight I was supposed to be on had vanished between Honolulu and Wake Island. That, it struck me, was why we were flying so low, so the crew could look for traces of the flight ahead of us. As far as I know, nothing was ever found.

Jim Johnson and I were both assigned to Ominato on Northern Honshu and spent a year working on the same radar crew. I was known as Eddie then, or Easy Ed because I liked to take things sort of easy. Today everyone calls me Gene, which has always been my family nickname.

Ron Weidner was part of the same crew but we didn't really become close friends until we met at the 511th reunion in Nashville in 1998. He says he stayed away from me at Ominato because I was such a screw-up, which is pretty true.

One night several of us (not including Ron) went into Ominato and did what we usually did and got drunk.

When the truck came to take us back to the site we refused to go and hired a couple of little cabs to take us to another town. When we got there we found some long, skinny bamboo sticks, like fishing poles, and went through town poking out all the streetlights. We just about had the town in total darkness before the local police caught us and threw us in jail.

We gave phony names like George Washington and Thomas Jefferson, which didn't fool the Japanese. Then, when the guards weren't looking, three of us broke out of the jail through a small window. I quickly became separated from the other two. Somehow I made it back to the site, all the way to my bunk -- and there was an AP waiting for me.

All of us were busted a grade. We also had to march around the flagpole for two hours a day wearing a 60-pound field pack loaded with rocks. Everyone not on duty was ordered to turn out and watch us. This went on for a week or two.

Another time I got in trouble when I lost my weapon on a courier run to Misawa. To this day I don't know what happened. But it got me in a lot of trouble.

The snow was something else. Coming from Alabama I'd never seen anything like it. When we'd go up the hill to go on duty, we tied ourselves together with a rope and walked on top of the snow. I don't know why we didn't sink in. When we got tired, we'd sit down on *top* of a telephone pole and rest.

It was also very windy. I only weighed 120 pounds or so and sometimes I'd be holding onto the rope between the buildings just a-flapping in the breeze.

The funny thing about all of this is that I've never had a job I enjoyed more. Working the scope. Plotting. Later I worked the ID desk and then worked with the officers in controlling aircraft.

I never wanted to leave. I loved Ominato and I would gladly have stayed for another two or three years. I even learned to like the condensed milk. When my final day came they had to carry me to the train.

After I left Ominato I never got in trouble again. I just seemed to get it out of my system. Before I left active duty, I was stationed at Norton Air Force Base in California and was named airman of the month several times. I even had a chance to go to OCS, although I'm sure no one who knew me at Ominato will believe that.

The electronic training I received in the Air Force shaped a lot of what I've done in civilian life. For many years I was a senior computer analyst with the Army Air Force Exchange Service. Then I went with NCR Corporation, where I was in charge of financial systems architecture and development.

I also spent several years managing hotels. I opened Residence Inn Hotels in Cincinnati and Winston-Salem and managed another in Louisville. Residence Inns were the first extended-stay type hotels.

Now my wife Joan and I manage a self-storage warehouse in Montgomery, Alabama until we decide to really retire.

Japan? I'd love to go back. Ron Weidner and his wife Jean have become good friends of ours and we still hear from Jim Johnson and his wife in Minnesota.

Gene Walker, 312 Air Base Blvd., Montgomery, AL 36108.
Phone 334/356-4410. Fax 334/262-6661.
e-mail: hedevil@knology.net

3

RIDING THE RAILS
TO A PLACE UNKNOWN

Herbert (Herb) Hancock
Radar Operator, Site 30, Rumoi,
and Site 2, Misawa
613th AC&W Squadron

I was a radar operator at Hilltop (Site 2) at Misawa when the first sergeant came to me one day in January 1949 and told me to get my bag packed and be in the orderly room at 0800 the following morning.

I was a Pfc. and I did what I was told without asking questions. When I got to the orderly room Major James Larson, commander of the 613th AC&W Squadron at Misawa, met me. There was a rail siding just a hundred yards from the orderly room and I had noticed a boxcar and flatcar, with a two and one-half ton truck and a weapons carrier on it.

Major Larson told me to get aboard the boxcar and guard it until he met me at the other end of the line. The boxcar was loaded with bunks and mattresses and furniture.

Major Larson said I was going to a radar site on Hokkaido but he never told me which one or where I was going.

I was given a carbine, two clips of ammunition, a canteen of water and enough K rations to last two or three days. The next thing I knew, an engine backed into the siding, hooked up the two boxcars with some others, and away we went.

I was 19 years old. I had joined the Air Force in 1948, right off the farm in Jackson County, near Scottsboro, Alabama, but I never expected anything like this. I had to slide the door of the boxcar back to let in some light. The snow outside was as high as the behind on a giraffe. I was nearly frozen from the cold wind blowing into the car and I was scared to death.

That night the train was put aboard the ferry for the trip across the strait from Northern Honshu to Hokkaido. Two Japanese workers discovered me in the boxcar and motioned for me to go up on deck. They were trying to be friendly, but my orders were to stay with the boxcar and that's where I stayed.

It was pitch black and scary. I got one of the mattresses and put it on the floor of the boxcar and found a couple of blankets and that was my bed. I sort of felt like a hobo, riding the rails during the Depression, which I remembered so well from growing up in a sharecropping family in Alabama.

The next morning the boxcar and the flatcar were unhooked from the train and placed on a siding at Hakodate, on the southern tip of Hokkaido. While I was there I was paid a surprise visit by a Sergeant Walker. He said he was from the Motor Pool at Chitose and had been told to come down and check on me. He told me the same thing Major Larson told me -- that he'd see me at the other end of the line. I asked him where that was and he said Rumoi. It was the first time I knew where I was going.

After the cars were hooked onto another train, we went to Sapporo and then to Asahigawa, a place somewhere up in the interior of Hokkaido. There the two cars were hooked to still another train and off we went again. Finally, about 10 o'clock that night, we got to the end of the line and, sure enough, there were Major Larson, Sergeant Walker and a Lieutenant Nighswenger, who I learned later was a radar maintenance officer and the site commander. I sort of figured out that Major Larson and Sergeant Walker got there before I did because they had taken a faster passenger train and passed me somewhere along the way.

So that was the end of the train ride but it wasn't the end of the trip. The three had come for me in a weasel but there was no room for me to sit inside. So I tied my duffel bag to the back of the weasel and lay down across the hood of the engine. And that's how I traveled the last two miles to the "clubhouse."

Life at Rumoi was really not bad. The clubhouse, as we called it, was a 10-room house that had once been occupied by a German scientist, or at least that's how the story went. We stayed there while our barracks was being completed at Site 30. An Air Force radio outfit also lived there. The house had steam heat and we had Japanese cooks and houseboys. I had never been waited on like that in my life.

We finally got the radar operational in the late spring of 1949, and I became the site's first radar operator. The radar was an old TPS-1B from World War II and I think the only thing we ever picked up on it was weather, snowstorms and a few birds.

I stayed at Rumoi until December 1949, when I was sent back to Misawa. I was at Site 2 until ADCC opened in June 1951. Altogether I spent 39 months and 16 days in Japan and was a staff sergeant when I left in September 1951.

After a year at Norton Air Force Base in California I was sent to Korea as NCOIC of Operations for the 607th AC&W Squadron. We were stationed just south of the 38th Parallel and could hear the big guns booming. We lived in tents and I've never wanted to camp out since.

While I was still in Japan I'd decided to make the Air Force my career and that's what I did, finally retiring as a chief warrant officer in 1970 after 22 years of active duty. Along the way I became an electronic warfare officer as well as being a surveillance officer and an aircraft controller.

Back home in Northeast Alabama I spent 23 more years as an employment interviewer and local office manager for the State of Alabama Department of Industrial Relations. Today, Mary, my wife of 46 years, and I live in Dutton, Alabama, within 10 miles of where I grew up.

Herb Hancock, 2299 County Road 18, Dutton, AL 35744-8741. Phone 256/228-3003. e-mail: hhancock@HIWAAY.net

4

A COLD BEER
FOR A COOL CHAPLAIN

James C. (Jim) Avery
Air Policeman, Site 34, Shiriya Saki
613th AC&W Squadron

I met Father Leonard Abercrombie, the Catholic chaplain, at the RTO in Ominato. It was a very hot summer day and while we were waiting for the truck to pick us up for the four and one-half hour drive back to our radar site at Shiriya Saki, Father Abercrombie said, "Jim, if you can take me to a cold beer, I'll buy."

So I led him down the street to a bar I was familiar with and ordered a couple of big, tall Japanese beers. Father Abby, who was making a tour of sites on Northern Honshu, really enjoyed it, so we ordered another round. The bar girls all thought he was kind of cute and started making a big fuss over him.

After a while he looked at me and said, "Jim, did you bring me to a house of ill repute?"

"I sure did," I replied, "but isn't the beer cold? What goes on in the back room isn't our concern."

He thought for a moment and said, "I guess you're right."

Ten years later I was at Maxwell Air Force Base in Alabama and I ran into a guy who was going to chaplain school. I asked him if he knew Father Abby and he said he was the chaplain at the VA hospital in Chicago. So I called him up and asked if he remembered me.

"Sure do," he said, "you're the one who took me to the whore house."

"That's right," I said, "but wasn't the beer cold?"

"That's the same thing you told me ten years ago," he laughed. I'm also Catholic and I always thought Father Abby was supposed to be saving us, but he insisted we had saved him. He also said we provided him with the fuel for a lot of sermons.

I was an air policeman at Site 34 and I always thought Shiriya Saki was a beautiful place. The site itself was at the foot of a mountain, right next to the ocean. The only problem was that the wind could get pretty fierce. One day it blew the cover completely off the radar while we were in an alert status tracking aircraft. The only way we could get the radar to turn in the wind was for four of us to get hold of it and physically push it around.

The radar actually was pretty primitive and was used for early warning only. Not long after I left in 1954, the site was replaced by Site 42, which had much newer equipment that came in with the Korean War.

But I'll never forget Site 34. One night three of us, Tony Smelgus, Ed Hval and I, returned to the barracks after watching a movie and stumbled onto another airman about to commit suicide. He was despondent over problems at home with his mother and was holding a carbine with a 30-round clip in it.

We were scared to death. We didn't want him to kill himself and we were also afraid he might kill us and others in the barracks if he pulled the trigger. We tried to talk to him. Then he started to move away, pointed the gun at himself, pulled the trigger and shot himself in the shoulder. Tony dove and grabbed the weapon before it hit the floor and could touch off additional rounds.

I grabbed the young man and tried to put pressure on his shoulder to stop the bleeding. Someone, I think it was Ed Hval, called the medics and the guy finally was airlifted out on an L-5.

The story, believe it or not, has a happy ending. The kid never returned to the site but he did return to active duty and went on to a successful career in the Air Force, finally retiring as a chief master sergeant.

I located one of the medics later and he said no one wanted to ruin the airman's life so the official report simply said that he had shot himself while cleaning his rifle. No one ever asked the three of us who were also in the room what happened.

When I got out of the Air Force I returned to Tarboro, North Carolina, where I grew up and used the GI Bill to get a degree in physical education from East Carolina University with the intention of becoming a football coach. After two years of coaching, I decided to become a public housing management officer for the U.S. Department of Housing and Urban Development and had a full career in

Atlanta, San Francisco, Chicago, Kansas City and Cincinnati. My wife Barbara and I now live in Dry Ridge, Kentucky and I still work a few days a week preparing funding grants for the city of Hamilton, Ohio, and make more money than I ever made before.

Jim Avery, 7 Angela Dr., Dry Ridge, KY 41035.
Phone 859/428-2011. e-mail: javery4207@aol.com

5

SITE 14 – WHERE
THE LIVING WAS EASY

Francis J. (Frank) Weiser
Ground Radio Maintenance
Site 14, Funagawa, and Site 33, Kamo
613th AC&W Squadron

Site 14 was the "country club" of the radar sites in northern Japan. The site was farther south than the others, so we didn't get as much snow and severe weather. And the living was pretty good--until the site was shut down and everything was moved to Site 33, about 15 miles away.

Site 14, sometimes referred to as Funagawa, was located on the west coast of northern Honshu, near the tip of a peninsula sticking out into the Sea of Japan. The site was only about 100 feet above sea level and sat right next to an old lighthouse.

Funagawa (which was later renamed Oga) served as a port for the Japanese navy in World War II and was actually some distance away. Nearby was the city of Akita and Japan's only oil wells. The Japanese used to tell us, "One day the B-29s came over and dropped bombs and the next day the war was over."

By the time I got there in 1954 all of that was history. The shoreline near the site was a national park and the pheasant hunting was great. We lived very comfortably in two-man cubicles inside a long building. The site commander, along with his wife and young son, lived in another building.

Japanese women served the tables in the mess hall and we paid $10 a month for someone to do our laundry, take care of KP duty and give us haircuts. We were pretty far out in the country and there was no one around except for the 60 to 80 of us at the site and a small number of Japanese who lived in the tiny village of Hatake right outside our main gate.

One time we ran out of eggs when the boxcar was late arriving in Funagawa with our monthly supply of food. We asked the Japanese to loan us 30 dozen fresh eggs to tide us over and promised to give them 60 dozen of our own eggs when our shipment arrived. What they didn't find out until it was too late was that the eggs they got from us had been in cold storage since the end of World War II. That ended the egg trading.

They also got even with us for kidding them about eating dog meat. One time some of them saw a side of mutton being unloaded from our boxcar at Funagawa and they started pointing at it and dancing around and yelling (in Japanese), "Dog meat! Dog meat!" It was pointless to try and argue.

But life at Site 14 was good and when it came time for us to move to Site 33 in the summer of 1955 no one really wanted to go. The problem with Site 14 was that its line of sight was pretty much blocked by mountains and hills on three sides, and about all we could track with our old World War II radar were ships in the Sea of Japan.

To get ready for the move, we were told to get rid of everything we didn't need and ship everything else to base supply at Misawa. This was my first hitch in the Air Force and I had no idea what I was supposed to do. So we started by throwing all of the old electronic parts for the radio and radar equipment into the back of a Six-By and hauled the stuff over to the bay and dumped it in. Everything else we tagged and shipped to Misawa.

Another thing we had to do before we left Site 14 was to take down the 90-foot radio antenna poles. Some of the guys, after a few drinks, used to like to climb the poles and do acrobatics. You can imagine how they felt when we loosened the guy wires and the poles immediately crashed to the ground because they were so rotted at the base.

From an operational standpoint, Site 33 was far superior to Site 14. The radome, and the radio transmitting and receiving towers, were all located high atop Mount Kamo and all of the equipment was new. Bunkers for operating the equipment were also on top of the mountain. But Site 33 was not nearly as pleasant a place to live as Site14 and none of us liked it.

The quonset hut where we lived was about halfway up the mountain and had pot bellied stoves to keep us warm. But the bunkers where we worked had no heat at all and we had to sleep on top of the equipment to keep warm during our 12 to 16-hour shifts.

Also, there were no latrines in the bunkers. There were chemical toilets but no one knew how to use them. So when we had to go, we just went outside, dropped our fatigues and did whatever we had to do. I'm just glad my tour ended and I was gone before the snow melted.

And it really did snow at Site 33, which seemed to get all of the snow that Site 14 didn't get.

We had two D-8 Cats on top of the mountain to try to keep the area cleared so we could get around but even they couldn't keep up with the snow. They also couldn't plow the road between where we lived and the top of the mountain, so we had to walk up the mountain. And each time we had to carry a five-gallon can of diesel fuel for the generators because there was no other means of transportation.

Getting back down to our quarters was another matter. We all wore these very long parkas and some of the guys would take the back of their parkas and pull it between their legs, then sit down in the snow and slide down the mountain. They thought it was safer that way. And also more fun.

I spent the rest of my first (but definitely not my last) visit to Japan at Site 33 and then decided to make the Air Force my career. I had grown up on a farm in northern Wisconsin and enlisted in the Air Force when I was 21. I retired as a master sergeant after 24 years of active duty, all of it in ground radio maintenance.

Shortly after I retired I had a heart attack. When I recovered from that I became a logistician, which is sort of a hopped-up supply man, for the Department of Defense and made 15 to 20 trips to Misawa between 1985 and 1993. On my last trip I took some extra time and drove through the mountains from Misawa, on the east coast of Honshu, to the peninsula where the two radar sites had been located. Everything at Site 14 was gone, even the little village of Hatake. At Kamo I could see a tower and a radome on top of the mountain and I'm pretty sure they were being operated by the Japanese Self Defense Force. But it was getting dark and I didn't try to drive up the mountain.

My last duty station in the Air Force was at Kelly Air Force Base in Texas and my wife Blanche and I still live in San Antonio so that I can be close to the Air Force hospital because of my heart condition. We have three sons and four grandchildren and I'm now fully retired.

Frank Weiser, 9734 Boonsboro, San Antonio, TX 78245-1908. Phone 210/675-1139. e-mail: yzr1@earthlink.net

6

SOMETHING'S THERE
. . . BUT WHAT IS IT?

Ronald Eugene (Ron) Weidner
Radar Operator, ADCC, Misawa
and Site 42, Ominato
39th Air Division and 613th AC&W Squadron

Some of the things we tracked on radar were unbelievable. We'd pick up blips going several thousand miles per hour. Then they would reverse direction or come to a dead stop.

We'd scramble F-100s and the pilots would see glowing, iridescent objects. They'd get close and the objects would vanish. Meanwhile, we'd be getting a hard radar signal and tracking everything the pilots were telling us. I remember one pilot in hot pursuit complaining in frustration, "I can't go any higher." Our scopes went to 65,000 feet and these objects would vanish, going straight up sometimes.

Do I believe in UFOs? Well, I don't know but there definitely was something there. The sightings seemed to run in cycles. We had physical radar printing something going faster than anything in the air then --or even today. We sent all of this information to higher headquarters, but we never knew what happened to it.

There were lots of strange things going on in Northern Japan in 1957 and 1958. Before I went to Site 42 at Ominato I spent six months at ADCC (Aircraft Direction Control Center) at Misawa. One of the things we had to do there was hand deliver orders for dispatch to the "outback" -- a radio communications center about six to eight miles away. The trip went past rows and rows of bunkers and through security checkpoint after checkpoint. I often wondered why such a deserted area had such heavy security. Later on I decided that it was a storage area for atomic weapons, but I never found that out for sure.

I definitely preferred Ominato to Misawa although I'll never forget the Christmas I spent at Misawa. Actually, it was Christmas Eve and I was a lonely, 17-year-old kid right off the farm in Genoa, Ohio. I was scheduled to work the midnight shift at ADCC but I wanted to go to church first. So I put on my dress blues and went -- all by myself. I sort of sensed something wasn't right when I entered the church. Everyone else was really dressed up and I didn't see many other airmen second class. Then the organ started playing, "Here Comes the Bride," and it dawned on me that I was in the wrong church. But everything turned out all right. I was invited to the reception and I even got to kiss the bride. Then I went to work.

While I was at Misawa I was on the base boxing team. I had been a Golden Gloves champion in Chicago before I entered the Air Force. I could have stayed at Misawa but I jumped at the chance to go to Ominato, even though it meant spending an additional six months overseas. It also separated me from my best friend, Len Tolman. He was from Salt Lake City and we met in basic training at Lackland. We went through radar school together at Keesler in Mississippi and then we both were assigned to ADCC at Misawa. I'm pretty sure he now lives in California.

Downtown Ominato in those days consisted of three bars, a public bathhouse, a railroad station, a few stores and more than enough girls to go around. For $50 a month you could have the girl of your choice, plus a house, and somehow she still managed to find beer money out of what was left over.

Of course, we didn't always go into town. I found another guy at the site who also knew how to play euchre and by the time I left we had everyone playing. We used chits and we'd bet against our next month's paychecks.

It was a good life all the way around. Here I was a kid, still in my teens, living like a millionaire. I had a houseboy who made my bed and shined my shoes. I never pulled KP. I never stood guard duty. I liked the people. I liked the work. I liked the money. And I liked the girls. Where else could a kid live like that?

After Japan I went back to Keesler and became an instructor in SAGE, which was an early form of computerized radar intercept control. With SAGE, you could pretty much fly the plane for the pilot. Unfortunately for the pilot, the system was based more on the parameters and capabilities of the aircraft than on those of the human body. One day I had a pilot pulling so many Gs he screamed, "Stop, you're slamming my teeth down my throat."

In civilian life I spent two years in charge of computer operations at Area 51 in Nevada. Then, unbelievably, I became city manager of Fernandina Beach, Florida, which turned out to be a lesson in small town politics I'll never forget.

For the last 35 years, I've been the owner of System Supplies, a business which I founded to provide computer supplies for businesses in Toledo and the northwest corner of Ohio.

My wife Jean and I live in Elmore, Ohio, and we've been to Alabama a couple of times and got together with Gene Walker, who also was at Ominato, and his wife Joan. I know Gene would like to go back to Japan and so would I. But I'm afraid the things I'd be looking for wouldn't be there anymore.

Ron Weidner, 1059 Celebration Drive,
Sebring, Fl 33872. Phone 863/471-3955.
e-mail: RonWei@aol.com

7

'HERE COMES THAT JOCK AGAIN'

Alfred O. (Al) Paul
Radar Operator, Site 2, Misawa
613th AC&W Squadron

I was working in a shoe factory in Merrill, Wisconsin, when I decided to join the Air Force right after it was officially formed in 1947. By the time I got to Misawa in March 1952 I was a staff sergeant with five years' experience as a "scope dope."

I was assigned to replace a master sergeant as NCOIC at ADCC (Air Defense Control Center). It was a pretty big leap in responsibility but I think everything would have worked out all right if I had not decided to try out for the Misawa football team. I didn't know that the captain who was operations officer hated sports and athletes. He told me, "I asked for you to be assigned here to be NCOIC, not to play football."

I told him I'd work nights or extra duty or whatever to get my job done but he wouldn't hear it and had me transferred to Radar Site 2 at Misawa, where I became one of four crew chiefs at "Hilltop," as the site was known. I made the football team as a backup quarterback but I only dressed out for home games – just to keep peace in the family.

My wife joined me at Misawa a year later and that was the end of my football playing for the base team. But I've always been a jock and still am – almost any sport and any position. I played football, baseball and basketball in high school, and throughout my 25 years in the Air Force I always played whatever I could wherever I happened to be.

In 1973, while I was stationed atop a mountain at Rolling Hills, California, I was named Athlete of the Year at nearby Fort McArthur, where we all were quartered. I played volleyball, softball, touch football, bowling and golf.

Today I live at the Armed Forces Retirement Home in Washington, D.C., where I moved after my wife died in 2003. And I'm still a nut about sports. I weigh 157 pounds, which is less than I weighed at Misawa. I play golf and have a 10-handicap and I always walk when I play. I have a 161 average in bowling. I also shoot pool, fish and play on the slow-pitch softball team. When people see me they always say, "Here comes that jock again." And the doctor here told me, "You have the best body of a 76-year-old I ever saw in my life.

Getting back to Misawa and Site 2 at "Hilltop," the operations complex was in a World War II Japanese bunker with approximately 120 cement steps almost straight down into the ground. We operated pretty much like any other site except that ADCC was only a half-mile away instead of being hundreds of miles distant, as was true with the other radar sites in northern Japan.

When an unknown target was detected a large orange light would flash constantly. ADCC would be notified and if the unknown target didn't meet certain criteria, our fighters would be scrambled to intercept the target – typically a Russian MIG fighter or a bomber checking our air defense capabilities. This cat and mouse game was never ending, with their aircraft usually staying on their side of the invisible dividing line in the sky and our aircraft staying on our side. When a pilot did stray across the line trouble broke out and it usually made front page news.

Those of us who manned the radar were known as "scope dopes," but we liked to remind ourselves that what we were doing contributed to the peace and comfort of everyone at Misawa – as well as the rest of the world.

I was at Misawa until September 1954 and despite the name Hilltop (which I never could figure out since the area was all pretty flat) it was one of only three assignments in my Air Force career which was not on top of a mountain. The other two were at Palermo, New Jersey (just outside of Ocean City) and at Hudson Bay, Canada.

After I retired from active duty I enrolled at Cypress College near Anaheim, California, and got my A.A. in business administration. Unbelievably, my wife Shirley and our daughter Carla and I all graduated on the same day in 1977, with Shirley and Carla both getting nursing degrees.

I spent 10 years as warehouse manager for a vending machine company serving southern California. Then my wife received an offer to become nursing administrator at a nursing home in Carson City, Nevada and we moved there. I became the central supply and transportation coordinator for the nursing home. Ten years later I retired for good from everything except sports.

We continued to live in Carson City until Shirley passed away. We had been married for 53 years. Our daughter Carla is now a lawyer in Reno; our son Robert is a clinical psychologist in Bowling Green, Kentucky, and our daughter Kimberly is a schoolteacher in Tacoma, Washington, and there are seven grandchildren.

*Al Paul, AFRH-W #71, 3700 N. Capitol St. NW, Washington, D.C. 20011-8400. Phone 1/202/291-3523.
e-mail alpaul@mymailstation.com*

8

THE 511TH AC&W GROUP--
Now You See It
. . . Now You Don't

Controversy and organizational confusion clouded much of the brief life span of the 511th Aircraft Control & Warning Group.

For five years, starting within a year after the end of World War II and extending until the late summer of 1951, all early warning facilities in Northern Japan were the responsibility of the 613th AC&W Squadron based at Johnson Air Base, near Tokyo.

This all changed on August 25, 1951, when the 511th was born at Misawa Air Base as part of a plan to expand the early warning coverage in what was termed the Northern Air Defense Area. The 613th, which had been a part of the 528th AC&W Group, also at Johnson, was reorganized and assigned to the 511th, with responsibility for Northern Honshu, and two new squadrons were created.

One of these, the 848th, was to be a companion squadron to the 613th responsible for the radar sites on Hokkaido. The other squadron, the 847th, was to be responsible for the Misawa Air Defense Control Center (ADCC).

In a little more than three years, the group and its squadrons grew to more than 1,500 airmen and officers and the new FPS-3 radar was proving of great value in the early warning defense network. What the radar wasn't prepared to detect, however, was the impending shutdown of the 511th. And on March 15, 1955, after an existence of just three years, six months and 22 days, the 511th vanished as quickly as it had arrived. The 847th AC&W Squadron also was deactivated while the 613th and 848th were placed under the direct command and control of the 39th Air Division at Misawa.

None of this was anticipated when the group was formed in 1951. Colonel George H. Sutherlin was group commander and for more than a year everything seemed to be progressing on schedule despite the seasonal weather battles and critical shortages of supplies, equipment and personnel. The 613th, with headquarters at Misawa, retained control of Site 14 at Funagawa, Site 34 at Ominato and Site 2 at Misawa, all on Northern Honshu. The sites on Hokkaido--Site 16 at Esashi, Site 18 at Wakkanai, Site 30 at Rumoi, Site 32 at Matsumae and Site 36 at Erimo-Zaki--which had previously been under the control of the 613th, now were a part of the 848th, headquartered at Chitose Air Base. The 847th at Misawa was responsible for the ADCC, which had been Site 2.

Suddenly, while all of this progress was being made, the group received an order in late 1952 to combine all administrative and logistical functions at the group headquarters at Misawa and to do away with the 848th headquarters at Chitose and the headquarters of the 613th and 847th at Misawa. The squadrons were reduced to a "one-and-one" status, which meant that each squadron would consist of one officer and one airman. This preserved the existence of the squadrons on paper in case a decision was made later to reactivate them (a wise move as subsequent events would prove).

Colonel Sutherlin vigorously protested the action, contending that the span of control would be too great for efficient management and supervision without supporting headquarters more closely related to the detachments. This, in turn, he argued, would reduce the over-all effectiveness of the 511th in carrying out its mission.

Despite his pleas, the reorganization went forward and by mid-December 1952 the squadrons had virtually ceased to exist. The workload at group headquarters immediately began to pile up beyond the capacity of the personnel to process it. Colonel Sutherlin's predictions proved accurate, so accurate, in fact, that exactly one year later, in December 1953, the 511th was directed to start reorganizing the three squadrons, complete with their own squadron headquarters.

Work began immediately to break down the consolidated personnel section and publish the necessary general orders. Through late in the day on New Year's Eve, work went on. Then a message was received cancelling the entire reorganization because it had not been approved by Headquarters USAF.

Support for re-establishment of the squadrons occurred again three months later, bolstered by the anticipated phase-in of Japanese Self Defense Force personnel. Finally in October 1954, with formal USAF approval still lacking, Fifth Air Force issued orders reactivating the three squadrons and maintaining the 511th Group headquarters. So, organizationally at least, everything was back the way it was 22 months earlier.

Meanwhile, the radar sites were going through major changes of their own. As new equipment improved the radar network, some of the older sites were phased out while newer ones were built.

When the squadrons were re-established in the fall of 1954, the 613th AC&W Squadron was given responsibility for Detachment 14 at Funagawa, Detachment 33 at Kamo and Detachment 37 at Kurosaki, all on Northern Honshu. The 848th was given responsibility for Detachment 18 at Wakkanai, Detachment 26 at Nemuro, Detachment 28 at Abashiri, Detachment 36 at Erimo-Zaki and Detachment 45 at Shikotsu, all on Hokkaido. Detachment 29 at Okushiri-Shima, an island in the Sea of Japan off the southwestern coast of Hokkaido, was first assigned to the 848th, then later to the 613th.

Detachment 26 at Nemuro, on the far eastern tip of Hokkaido, was phased in on November 14, 1951. Detachment 29 at Okushiri-Shima became operational in February 1952, and Detachment 28 at Abashiri was activated in April 1952, all with newer and better equipment and facilities.

Detachment 45 at Shikotsu, north of Sapporo on Hokkaido, was activated in October 1953 and became the headquarters of the 848th when the squadrons were

41

reactivated in 1954. Detachment 33 at Kamo, on the northwest coast of Honshu, was organized and occupied in April 1954 and led to the closing of Detachment 14 at Funagawa.

Three sites were discontinued as no longer needed in the radar defense network: Site 34 at Shiriya Saki, Honshu, in November 1953; Site 32 at Matsumae, Hokkaido, in April 1954, and Site 30 at Rumoi, Hokkaido, in February 1955.

Detachment 42 later replaced Detachment 34 at Ominato and became the headquarters of the 613th AC&W Squadron, and Detachment 37 was built at Kurosaki, Honshu.

When the 1954 reorganization took place, all of the radar sites were assigned to the 49th Fighter Bomber Wing at Misawa for logistical support. In early 1955, responsibility for support of all of the detachments on Hokkaido and Detachment 29 at Okushiri-Shima was assigned to the 4th Fighter Wing at Chitose. An administrative detachment of the 848th was set up at Chitose to serve in a liaison capacity between the 4th Fighter Wing and the 848th and its detachments.

All of these changes were part of an over-all master plan, called Project Airtight, to equip the early warning sites with the new FPS-3 radar and other up-to-date equipment, and to build more permanent facilities to house both equipment and personnel.

The plan was successful and with each new installation the organization's ability to make radar pickups and intercepts increased. One report said that during the latter part of 1954 the 511th "could boast the highest on-the-air time in the Japanese Air Defense Force and Fifth Air Force" while carrying out its mission "of continuous radar surveillance and training to sustain a high degree of efficiency in the identification, control and assistance to aircraft navigation in our area of responsibility."

As the 511th prepared to enter 1955, the outlook was bright. Colonel Steve J. Gadler was group commander, having succeeded Colonel John A. H. Miller, who previously had succeeded Colonel Sutherlin.

Under Colonel Gadler the group headquarters was streamlined and a stepped-up program of assistance to the radar detachments was initiated. The FPS-3 continued to show proficiency in tbe early warning defense structure. Tilt tests, radar evaluation tests and a project to pinpoint the exact location of the radar sites were all being carried out.

The biggest problem was the communications system within the Northern Air Defense Sector, which was proving inadequate to handle all of the operational and administrative traffic. Work continued on an FM expansion program but circuit outage problems and frequency blocks at Sasayama and Toyoni-Dake relays slowed the progress as did the isolated conditions caused by the heavy snowfall.

And then, in less than 30 days, the 511th passed out of existence.

On February 20, 1955, a message was received from Fifth Air Force reducing all aircraft control and warning groups to a one-and-one status pending final deactivation on March 15. The responsibilities of the 511th were to be absorbed by the 39th Air Division at Misawa. The 613th and 848th AC&W squadrons were placed under the direct command and operational control of the division. The 847th AC&W Squadron was ticketed for deactivation on March 15. Colonel Gadler, the group commander, was named Division Director of Materiel.

The immediate reaction was one of shock and disappointment since the group appeared to be achieving its goals. As the final few weeks raced by, some of the wisdom behind the move began to surface. Since the reorganization of the group six months earlier, more and more responsibilities had been delegated to the squadrons for operations, administration, personnel and supplies. The Fifth Air Force order could be perceived as the next step in this direction, by eliminating the group as an intermediate, and unnecessary, level of command.

Another apparent advantage was a clearer delineation of responsibility in the operational control of the AC&W squadrons. On many occasions, the command control of the squadrons exercised by the 511th overlapped the operational control exercised by the 39th. This was particularly true with the Air Defense Control Center (ADCC) operated by the 847th AC&W Squadron at Misawa. In one swift move, the Fifth Air Force order eliminated the 847th and placed the ADCC totally under the control of the 39th Air Division. And any overlapping related to the 613th and 848th was removed by eliminating the 511th.

By March 3, less than two weeks after the message was received, the group headquarters was vacated and all personnel were in place at division headquarters. Twelve days later the 511th AC&W Group and the 847th AC&W Squadron were officially placed on an inactive status, never again to play a role in the air defense of Northern Japan.

Most of the information in this summary of the 511th was obtained from the "Final History, 511th Aircraft Control & Warning Group, APO 919," prepared by First Lieutenant Jean E. Phillips upon the group's deactivation in 1955. Lieutenant Phillips was the group's adjutant and historical officer.

9

PREPARING THE WAY
FOR THE RADAR SITES

Teruo Nishijima
Interpreter and Advisor
Site 16, Esashi; Site 32, Matsumae;
Site 34, Ominato; Site 36, Erimo-Zaki;
Site 26, Nemuro; Site 28, Abashiri;
Site 29, Okushiri Shima and
Site 45, Ishikari Tobetsu

The first time I knew anything about American radar sites being built on Hokkaido was in August 1947, two years after the war had ended. I was a Hokkaido government employee in Muroran and was transferred to Esashi, on the southwest coast of Hokkaido. My job was to serve as liaison between the government and the U. S. occupational forces which were building permanent housing for a radar installation in Kaminokuni, about five miles away where they had a small building with the radar. The main forces were staying in Esashi. While I was there I heard of other radar installations at Wakkanai and Rumoi.

About a year later, the permanent barracks were completed at Kaminokuni but the site was still referred to as the Esashi detachment. Later it was changed to Kaminokuni and at some point, perhaps in 1950, the site number was changed from 13 to 16.

A major change for me occurred in April 1949 when I quit my government job and was employed by the Americans as site interpreter. I had studied English in school in Japan but during the war the teaching of English was prohibited by the Japanese government. The use of English also was discouraged but I kept learning it because it was my hobby.

When the war was over, the Hokkaido government recruited interpreters to assign to major police stations. The examinations were so competitive that only one of every 100 or 200 applicants was accepted. I made it and gave up my schoolteacher's job and was sent to Muroran.

It is interesting that while Japan prohibited the teaching of English, the U.S. Army was training Japanese language specialists. They shortened the Pacific war just as the American use of radar did.

When the Korean War broke out in June 1950, even greater emphasis was placed on establishing the radar sites in Northern Japan. One day in July of that year, Lt. Harold Barclay, the Site 16 commander, took me on a Jeep trip with him under strict orders to tell no one where we had been. It turned out (I think can reveal this now) that we went to Matsumae, where personnel had just arrived to begin constructing Site 32. It was a clear, hot day and we stayed in an old building used by a Japanese army radar unit during the war. The U.S. personnel stayed there until permanent barracks were built nearby. Lt. John Bon Tempo from Misawa supervised the opening of the site and the first site commander was Captain Olsen.

About a month after my trip to Matsumae I was sent on TDY to Shiriya Saki on the northern tip of Honshu for the construction of Site 34. At the town of Ominato I was joined by site personnel who had flown in from Misawa and we went to Shiriya Saki by truck and put up tents down the hill. I helped employ Japanese workers, served as interpreter and was sort of a jack-of-all-trades and master of none. The weather was pretty hot and it was very hard to transport the construction materials to the top of the hill where the radar site was being built.

To make matters worse, every night we were under attack by a winged enemy -- not Russian MIGs, but mosquitoes by the millions. Lt. Bon Tempo supervised the work there, too, and Captain Fred Hutchins became the first site commander.

In June 1951, I was similarly involved in the construction of Site 36 at Erimo-Zaki, on the south coast of Hokkaido. An LST unloaded the radar equipment on the beach several miles south of the site. The first personnel took a train to the end of the line at Samanai, several miles north of the site. From there we took a truck to a spot near a lighthouse and built prefab housing. After rounding up some Japanese personnel I returned to Site 16. Lt. Bon Tempo, again, was in charge of the work at Site 36 and Captain Young was the first site commander.

Site 26 at Nemuro came next, in October 1951, and the procedure was somewhat different. Captain Joseph Leadingham, the first site commander, and his men and I took an overnight train from Sapporo to Nemuro.

When we got there the next day, we entered the second floor of a big building annexed to City Hall and proceeded to make a big hole in the roof to install the radar. This upset the city authorities. The U.S. occupation of Japan had ended just one month earlier and it seemed that neither the U.S. forces nor the Japanese government had bothered to notify local officials about what was going to happen.

Interestingly, we learned that many years earlier the building had been the site of a party given for Charles Lindbergh and his wife when they visited Japan on a worldwide tour after he had become the first person to fly solo across the Atlantic Ocean.

From our standpoint, we found the building to be very cold even though we put in oil heaters. We also had difficulty finding skilled Japanese such as carpenters and electricians. But we finally found some and I went back to Site 16 until April 1952, when I was sent to Abashiri.

The first site personnel and I traveled to Abashiri by train and stayed at a hotel for a few days. We put up tents near the lighthouse outside the city, which prompted a protest from the landlady who said she could not understand why Americans should occupy the land without any notice or her consent. A meeting was held in the mayor's office and a captain from the site apologized and said he was just obeying orders and that he thought all necessary action had been taken with the Japanese government about using the land.

Things were finally worked out and the site personnel stayed in the tents until permanent buildings were ready nearby.

As usual, my job ended with the hiring of Japanese personnel and I returned to Site 16. I believe Major Edwin Murrill was the first commander at Site 28.

Right after I got back to Esashi, Site 16 was closed and I was sent to Okushiri Shima, an island off the southwest coast of Hokkaido, where a radar installation had just opened on top of the highest mountain. Transportation between the beach town of Okushiri and the site was a real problem and for a long time the only means of transportation was a bulldozer. Captain Arthur Jehli was the first site commander.

While at Site 29, I heard about the new headquarters being built for the 848th AC&W Squadron at Tobetsu, not far from the capital of Hokkaido in Sapporo. I asked Major French who was then the site commander, for a transfer and he was kind enough to oblige. I arrived in June 1954 just as Site 45 was opening and that was my home base for the next five and one-half years.

For a long time there was a great deal of confusion over the name for the site. At first the site was called Shikotsu. This was probably a clerical mistake since there was a place called Shikotsu near Chitose, where a site had been considered. In fact I remember visiting there once with a survey team. In reality, Site 45 was atop Mount Asoiwayama near the town of Tobestsu and in later years the site officially became known as Asoiwayama Air Station.

Lt. Col. Nolan Hatcher arrived in October 1954 and became the first 848th squadron commander. He promoted me from interpreter to advisor, the top job title, and I was very happy. In January 1955, Captain Masahito Seiko arrived with the first contingent of Japanese Air Force personnel to begin training to take over the site.

Site 45 was officially deactivated as a U.S. outpost in December 1959 and its operation was turned over to the Japanese. The last two U.S. representatives there were a supply sergeant, whose name I'd give anything to remember, and me. I prepared my own discharge document, addressed to the Hokkaido government, and the supply sergeant signed it on behalf of the U.S. Air Force detachment.

I was released effective January 18, 1960, contrary to my original expectation that the occupation of Japan by U. S. troops would last at least half a century. Fortunately, I was re-employed by the Hokkaido government in April of that year. Since then I have lived in Sapporo.

I'm often asked if the radar sites are still on Hokkaido. They are and the Japanese Air Force even uses the same site numbers.

Teruo Nishijima, 1-4-18 Asabucho, Kitaku, Sapporo, 001-0045, Japan. Phone 011-736-6659.

10

NO COMPLAINTS
AND NO COMPLIMENTS

Nolan C. Hatcher
Commander, 848th AC&W Squadron
Site 45, Ishikari Tobetsu

Colonel Steve Gadler was the last commander of the 511th AC&W Group, headquartered at Misawa. And everyone who remembers him, or who has ever heard of his reputation for being tough to get along with, is amazed when I say that he and I got along just fine.

Before I became the first commander of the 848th AC&W Squadron in September 1954, I spent a couple of months as deputy commander of the 511th at Misawa. I was sent to Site 45 just before Colonel Gadler arrived in Japan but I served directly under him and we became very good friends.

He was a technician; I was a musician and an educator. He was strong in technical matters, math and physics. I was strong in history and the humanities. But we both were of the same conservative political persuasion and that helped us get along. When I was ready to leave Japan at the end of 1955, he and his wife invited me to spend Christmas with them in their home near Fuchu, outside Tokyo. But that's getting ahead of the story.

I was commander of the 848th for 14 months and I'm still proud of the job everyone did in keeping the Cold War cold.

The weather, of course, was our major problem. I was born and raised in Texarkana, Texas, and I had never encountered anything like a Hokkaido winter with over 300 inches of snow on top of a ridge of mountains.

Another major problem, although not everyone knew it at the time, was communicating with the headquarters staff of the 511th Group at Misawa, which was supposed to be supporting our radar sites on Hokkaido. In fact, that was their MISSION. To be truthful, we had a painful relationship which did not get any better as time moved on. For example, once we submitted a requisition for snow shovels and the response was a shipment of lawn mowers. Other examples could be cited regarding the Department of Logistics and Chaplain Services, but this would serve no useful purpose.

On March 15, 1955, the 511th was deactivated on short notice by order of the Fifth Air Force. I was invited to Misawa for the final few days, which were celebrated with an "Irish Wake," complete with green beer.

For those of us at Site 45, which was the headquarters of the 848th on Hokkaido, life went on pretty much as it had except that we now reported directly to the 39th Air Division at Misawa. Its commander was Colonel Elder. Several staff members of the old 511th moved over to the headquarters of the 39th Air Division. One of them was Lt. Col. John (Pete) Petrovich, the director of Radar Operations. Without doubt, Pete was the most effective and most supportive of any of the Misawa officers that we dealt with. He personally visited all of our sites regularly and was always available by telephone—day or night, all seasons.

Our radar mission in the 848th was sorted out according to the equipment that was installed at each site. The smaller sites around the perimeter of Hokkaido were there for early warning (EW). At Site 45, we had Bendix and General Electric radars that served us for ground control intercept and ground control approach (GCI/GCA). We worked hand-in-hand with the pilots of the 4th Fighter Wing at nearby Chitose Air Base and with other aircraft, as needed. We also called in our other aircraft contacts to higher radar controlling authority at Misawa.

Several non-military personnel helped considerably in meeting our mission requirements. There was Mr. Gomez, our first Bendix tech rep; Jack Aback, also from Bendix; Roger Wolf, a Philco tech rep (and an ex-Marine officer); "Tex" Brehm, a Cummins Diesel tech rep, and Pete Harding, who was with RCA. Roger Wolf is known to many today for keeping up with all of the ex-members of the 848th and other outfits and helping to guide our annual reunions.

As I think back on my time as commander of the 848th I never cease to be greatly impressed with the high caliber of the men we had. Although we had two fires at our eight sites, we never lost a single man. We never had a desertion, an AWOL, a suicide or a loss of life from any cause. We also never had a unit or serviceman honored or decorated for distinguished service or heroism. We simply did our jobs and served our tours of duty, without the accompaniment of our dependents, without complaint—and without compliment.

After Japan, I was assigned to the headquarters of the Military Air Transport Command at Andrews Air Force Base, Maryland. From there we moved to Scott Air Force Base, Illinois, then to Wheelus Air Force Base at Tripoli, Libya, and then back to Scott AFB. I was retired in June 1967, as a command pilot, with approximately 6,000 flying hours. My last flying experience was in Lockheed T-33 single engine jets.

Going back a bit, I entered the U.S. Army Air Corps as an aviation cadet at Harlingen, Texas, in August 1941. I was commissioned a second lieutenant and rated as a military pilot in 1942. My first officer assignment was as a pilot instructor at the Columbus Army Advanced Flying School in Mississippi. On my first night there, May 1, 1942, I met Willetta Marion, a senior at Mississippi State College for Women. We were married four months later and have remained so for 61+ years. She is the mother of our three children and has been my faithful companion for three careers, including the 22 years after retiring from the Air Force.

In 1970, I received my doctorate in education from Auburn University to go along with my previous degrees from Abilene Christian University and the University of Oklahoma. I had previously graduated from several schools of the Air University (Air Tactical School, Academic

Instructor School, Air Command and Staff College in Communications, and the Air War College).

Following my doctoral graduation, I remained on the faculty of Auburn for four years. Then Troy State University in Troy, Alabama, initiated a new program to provide educational development for European servicemen and their dependents. I was invited to join the overseas faculty of TSU in Germany, where I later became coordinator of the program until joining the faculty on the main campus in 1974. I was promoted to full professor and later dean of the College of Special Programs (overseas mainly) until my retirement, with 22 years of service, in September 1989. Most of the remaining years have found me in a third profession, as a private investor.

In 1985, I had the enjoyable experience of returning to Tobetsu and Site 45. This time, Willetta joined me and we were treated royally. Major Seiko (now colonel, retired) and his wife met us in Tokyo, showed us around and treated us to dinner with former members of his staff. Then we journeyed to Hokkaido where we were met by Teruo Nishijima, my one-time advisor/interpreter with the 848th Squadron.

Nishijima-san influenced the Governor of Hokkaido to proclaim "Hatchers Day" while we were there, with free admission to all government museums. At Site 45, the JASDF commander asked us to take the review and inspect his personnel. We were extremely flattered and most appreciative of this special kindness and honor.

My assignments during World War II and the Korean War were difficult but rewarding, but I shall never forget the

848th AC&W Squadron and the Island of Hokkaido for the wonderful people I was with.

Nolan C. Hatcher, 209 Norfolk Ave., Troy, AL 36081. Phone: 334/566-6886. e-mail: nhatcher@troycable.net.

11

SPACE CADET
AND HIS VISIT TO WAKKANAI

Richard (Dick) Waldron
Radio Operator, Site 18, Wakkanai
848th AC&W Squadron

Space Cadet and I first met during a radio
transmission one morning in May 1953 while I was on duty
at the remote direction finding station at Wakkanai.

"Air Force 6563 calling Wakkanai Dog Fox. Over."
"Roger, Air Force 6563," I responded.
"This is Wakkanai Dog Fox. Go ahead."
"Request bearing to your station. Over."
"Roger, bearing zero six eight. Got any mail? Over."
"Ah-roger, bearing zero six eight. Yes, two bags.
Over."
"All-riiiight!! Air Force 6563 this is Wakkanai Dog
Fox. The limo is waiting at the strip. See you soon. Over."
"Ah-roger."

The small, single-engine courier plane was a distant speck moving over the low mountains before gradually assuming shape as it got closer. Air Force 6563 then circled the dirt and gravel airstrip and slowly bounced to a landing. On board were the military pilot and one passenger, someone wearing civilian clothes who we later found out was a special visitor from Washington.

Usually just an enlisted man or two and a Japanese guard met the infrequent courier planes but this time the commanding officer, the "Old Man," went along.

Mail sacks and some official bags were unloaded from the plane to the jeep and the Japanese policeman was posted to the first shift to guard the L-20. Then the others crowded into the open jeep and drove back to the site.

Later, after the mail had been distributed and the civilian had been closeted with the Old Man, the pilot showered, ate, and dropped into The Barn, an old building that had been made into a combination recreation room, theatre and bar.

There he got to talking with a few of the off-duty men hanging around and playing ping-pong. The pilot, a second lieutenant, seemed to fit in right away. He was only 22 but still a little older than most of the others. He had a pleasant and personable way about him and it later came out that he had been married for a year and was going to become a father within a few weeks. But he wouldn't be able to see his new son or daughter for another year due to his overseas tour.

He had not brought any extra clothing with him because he expected to be back at his air base the next day.

So he showed up in the rec room in his flight suit. The enlisted guys, all dressed in fatigues, good-naturedly named him Space Cadet after a cartoon character of that name. It stuck.

The first night Space Cadet was at the site there wasn't much doing at the bar but he and a bunch of guys sat around telling stories, laughing and having a few beers. He was an officer and they were enlisted men but rank wasn't a factor. They were simply friends drinking socially in a far off land with mutual respect based on their capabilities and jobs.

The next day Space Cadet wandered about the site, chatting easily with those he met. The second night, still in his flight suit, he again dropped into The Barn, this time to watch a movie he had brought. The movie was a two-year-old, three-reeler, and when the portable screen was put up on the ping-pong table and the lights turned off, the rec room became the theatre, with the informal atmosphere enhanced by the haphazard location of the chairs.

Each movie reel was shown in turn, rewound, and the next reel loaded and shown, thus resulting in two major intermissions. This allowed time to visit the latrine or get a fresh beer or coke at the bar.

There were pretty girls in some movie scenes and their appearance produced frequent yells of "FOCUS!", "BACK-IT-UP!" and "SHOW THAT PART AGAIN!" When the film broke or got stuck and bubbled up with brown spots, boos and shouts of "WHAT THE HELL DID YOU DO NOW?" were followed by multiple calls of "LIGHTS!"

It was raucous fun and Space Cadet joined in the laughter with his own comments and complaints. Afterward he and a few guys stopped at the bar in the next room for a beer before hitting the sack.

The third day was a repetition for Space Cadet, and he passed the time waiting for the civilian to finish his meetings by playing ping-pong in the rec room and drinking coffee in the mess hall. Someone suggested a party that night, but early in the afternoon the civilian finally finished his business with the Old Man, and Space Cadet and his passenger had to leave for another site down the coast, stay overnight, and return to Misawa the following day.

A few guys in a carryall followed the jeep to the airstrip to see the courier plane leave and everyone was a little sad when Air Force 6563 took off. They all watched as Space Cadet buzzed the site, wiggled his wings, and climbed into the clouds. The party could wait. Space Cadet would be back.

Since radio operators rotated shifts at different jobs at the site, my turn happened to come up for a day shift at the main radio room the day after Space Cadet left. It was a dull afternoon and I put my headset half on my ears and half on my temples as I monitored a couple of radio frequencies. I leaned back in the chair and put my hands behind my head. As I looked out the window over the sandbags at the cloudy sky I thought there could be some weather coming.

I listened to Morse Code and logged the sporadic transmissions. Then I heard one of the other sites, Site 28 at Abashiri, call Misawa with a priority message. I was bored and looking for something to do so I copied the encrypted text and decoded it. It read:

Air Force 6563 crashed on takeoff this site x
no survivors x
request helicopter remove four bodies x

I sat there stunned.

I was at Wakkanai from June 1952 to September 1953 and Space Cadet remains one of my most vivid memories. I had joined the Air Force in January 1951 with five of my friends from Boston, had basic training at Lackland, was assigned as a clerk-typist at Nellis in Las Vegas, played for the Nellis baseball team, and transferred to the 32-week radio operator school at Keesler in Biloxi, Mississippi.

Six of us from the Keesler class were assigned to sites on Hokkaido, and I went to Site 18 at Wakkanai. Once there Major Haines volunteered me to get a ham radio license and a MARS (Military Amateur Radio System) license. After 15 months at Wakkanai, I talked my way into a transfer to Misawa to start a MARS radio station at 511th Headquarters. While working in the MARS station I also played on the Misawa football team and the Misawa baseball team.

My four-year AF enlistment ended with 25 months in Japan. On returning home I went to the University of Massachusetts and got a degree in business. I then spent many years in data processing and computer sales and, after a layoff, tried self-employment. When nothing significant happened, I "ran away to sea" as a radio officer in the merchant marine. I joined my first ship at age 45 and sailed for 13 years.

I sailed on various types of vessels (about a dozen containerships; three oil research ships; an oil tanker; a roll-on, roll-off vehicle ship; a WWII Caine Mutiny-type cargo ship, and a fish factory trawler). There were 60 Atlantic crossings, 15 Pacific crossings, two round-the-world trips, and visits to 33 countries.

Since "coming ashore" I wrote a book in 1994 called "Futures 101: An Introduction to Commodity Trading," which is still in bookstores in 2005.

I married, had a son and daughter, and was widowed. I remarried, had two more sons and two grandchildren, and now live in Quincy, Massachusetts, happily married to Polly.

Dick Waldron, 54 Monmouth St., Quincy, MA 02171-1048.
Phone 617/328-4210. Fax 617/328-0050
e-mail:dickwaldron@attbi.com

12

HOW TO SURVIVE AS A KAMIKAZE PILOT

Raymond S. (Ray) Bergen
Radar Operator, Site 36, Erimo-Zaki
848th AC&W Squadron

Training the JASDF personnel to take over the air defense mission was a pretty good job.

The Japanese soaked everything up and were eager to learn. One of the most interesting things was to quiz the officers and NCOs as to what they had done during World War II, since most all of them were retreads.

One of the officers told us that he had been a kamikaze pilot. When we asked him why he was still with us his answer was, "Fortunately, war end before I solo."

When I arrived at Detachment 36 in March 1957 there were about 40 USAF personnel. When I left in May 1958 there were 11. As the number of Americans dwindled, all of the EMs were billeted in what had been the NCO barracks. That left us with that building; the officer billets; the Airman's Club, to which everyone, including the officers, belonged, and the combination mess hall, PX, dispensary and Orderly Room. I think that we also kept a small supply building and a secure area in the radio shack. The Japanese had the rest of the station.

Because there were so few of us, just about everyone had his own "private" vehicle. I had a weasel -- the little tracked buggy that was great on sand but terrible on snow. TSgt. Russ Harbaugh, the operations NCOIC, had a jeep and our operations officer, Lt. Arthur Sullivan, had a weapons carrier with a squeaky brake so you always knew when he showed up on the hill. Lt. Sullivan was a Notre Dame graduate.

Since the main idea was for the JASDF to take over the air defense system, the five of us in operations were kept busy. In the beginning, when we had more people, there was always an American on duty but later on, as we lost people, we would just have somebody on the hill during the day and until about 2000. We were only about five minutes away when we were in the club or barracks. The only time it was mandatory that there be USAF personnel on the hill was when the RB-29 "weather" flights from Johnson AB were passing through on their runs up north to the Russian coast.

In addition to my radar duties, I also ran the PX for an extra $30 a month, which was big bucks then. The situation with the Airman's Club was even more interesting.

When got to the site there was about $4,000 in the club account with Chase-Manhattan's Chitose AB Branch. Someone found out that when all USAF personnel left the site, the club would shut down and all of the money on deposit in the bank would revert to the Airman's Club at Chitose.

When this was discovered, every effort was made to use up as much of the surplus as possible. The club started paying for everything- -houseboys and girls; laundry service; the barber, and, in the mess hall, a KP, a Japanese cook and two waitresses who doubled as masseuses two days a week. Yes, masseuses. Everything was on the up-and-up. They would put a couple of tables together, throw a mattress on top and give massages.

The club also paid for extra food in the mess, such as Kobe beef and Wakkanai crabs. When I left there was still close to $1,000 in the account. No matter how hard we tried, the club kept making money. The JASDF troops, especially the officers, were our best paying customers.

When the spring of 1958 came, Sergeant Harbaugh and I were due to rotate home at the same time but we both had to spend six extra weeks at the site waiting for our replacements to show up from Misawa.

Erimo-Zaki was not my first Air Force assignment nor was it my first time in Japan. I spent a year in Korea in 1955 and got a good look at Japan during a couple of R & Rs. I enlisted in the Air Force in January 1952 at age 17 after leaving high school a little early. I passed both the high school and college level GEDs and enrolled at the College of Great Falls in Great Falls, Montana in 1954 under the auspices of the Operation Bootstrap program. At that time I was only a year behind my high school peers.

After Erimo-Zaki I spent another four years on active duty, most of it at McChord AFB just outside of Tacoma, Washington. Altogether I had 10 years in the Air Force when I finally got out.

I thought I wanted to be an air traffic controller in civilian life but the pressure of attending the FAA school cured me of that. I had learned to write computer programs while in the Air Force's SAGE system and computers became my life for the next 40 years. I worked for several different companies and then spent the last nine years as a private computer consultant.

When I retired in 2001 my wife Barbara and I were living in Southern California. We both wanted to get out of the Los Angeles area and moved first to Eugene, Oregon and then later to Vancouver, Washington.

Ray Bergen, 13210 SE Seventh St., #71, Vancouver, WA 98683-6931 Phone 360/828-9640 e-mail: brbergen@attbi.com

13

THE DOWNING OF AN RB-29
AT NEMURO

George M. (Dobey) Lynch
Aircraft Controller, Site 26, Nemuro
848th AC&W Squadron

On our scopes we watched the RB-29 making strip photos of Hokkaido. As it headed east on one pass it flew directly over us, heading toward the most easterly point of land.

The MIGs in the Soviet-held Kuriles scrambled as they always did when one of our aircraft came within 100 miles. We lost the RB-29 in our ground clutter and then we heard the May Day call on the radio.

At the eastern end of Hokkaido, the MacArthur Line, which separated us from the Soviets, was so close that there was no room for the RB-29 to turn port and head back west. But turn port the pilot did and that's when the MIGs jumped him, blowing away the tail section of the plane.

We guessed that the crew had bailed out east of us so Major French went out with a search party. They found 10 of the 11 crew members about 10 miles away, delirious with joy when our trucks appeared. They thought they had landed in the Kuriles, which would have resulted in a mysterious disappearance for all of them.

The only one who didn't make it was the photographer. He was a little guy, maybe 125 pounds, and the wind evidently carried him into some rocks just off shore. Our men found him drowned and under water, still in his chute harness next to one of the rocks.

By six that night, the survivors were all at our site, where we fed them and gave them some whiskey. About 9 o'clock a helicopter flew in and took them to an airfield at Kenebetsu, about 40 miles from Nemuro, and from there they were flown back to Yokota Air Base.

For us at the radar site, the aftermath was worse than the event. We wrote statements and had paperwork out the ears for days afterward. The incident happened on November 7, 1954, and made all of the papers in the U.S. One account said the RB-29 was the sixth U.S. plane shot down by the Soviets in that part of the world in three years.

It's interesting that in my 17 months at Nemuro I can never recall our radar operators picking up any Russian aircraft crossing the MacArthur Line. On the other hand, about once a month orders would come up from down south: "Stop reporting." That meant we should not record what we were seeing on our scopes. We soon learned that was the clue to look to the southwest and soon, coming at top speed, would be what must have been a photo recon plane at about 40,000 feet, heading over us toward the Kurile Islands. A little later it would come hightailing back before the MIGS could scramble and get up to altitude.

I also had the misfortune to be involved in a minor, but tragic, way in another major news event -- the sinking of the Toya Maru on September 26, 1954. Our site commander leading up to that time was Major Angus Hopkins, a 48-year-old reserve officer recalled to active duty some four years earlier and sent to God-forsaken Nemuro. He had twin daughters, born after he departed from somewhere in Virginia and he had never seen them.

One of my additional duties at the site was that of Transportation Officer, since I knew how to type. When Major Hopkins' departure from Site 26 became imminent he corralled me and insisted that the travel orders I was to prepare would call for him to board a train to Hakodate rather than to Chitose. The idea was that instead of flying from Chitose to Tachikawa, as everyone else did who was homeward bound, he would take a train to Hakodate, then take the train ferry across the strait to Aomori on northern Honshu, and proceed to Tokyo by rail.

I balked. He became furious, as was his bent. He outranked me and, discretion being the better part of valor, I relented and cut the orders the way he wanted. The decision cost him his life, much to my everlasting regret.

A typhoon struck Hakodate just as the Toya Maru was departing and the ferry went down with the loss of nearly 1,500 lives. I often wonder about the major's twins, now approaching age 50. Despite all of his bluster, Major Hopkins would have been a magnificently devoted father.

Dobey Lynch died on March 23, 2002, a few weeks after providing the information for the preceding account. He was a practicing attorney in Latrobe, Pennsylvania, at the time of his death. Dobey was a graduate of Penn State and received his law degree at the University of Pittsburgh. He and his wife Dorothy had three children and four grandchildren.

14

THE GREAT ABASHIRI
SNOWSTORM OF 1957

Fred Young
Radar Maintenance, Site 28, Abashiri
848th AC&W Squadron

As far as I know, I am the only person to have experienced both the great Abashiri snowstorm and fire of March 1957 and the devastation of Florida's Hurricane Andrew in August 1992.

The Abashiri snowstorm was absolutely the worst I ever saw. It started with a light but steady snowfall on Saturday, March 9 and went on until the following Sunday—eight days later. I remember it like it was yesterday.

I was getting ready to go on leave to Sapporo, Misawa and Tokyo and had withdrawn $195 from the Orderly Room safe and secured it in my barracks locker. I went to bed Wednesday night with the snow still coming down and was sound asleep about 1:30 in the morning when someone burst into the barracks yelling, "Fire, fire," and turned on the lights.

Smoke was billowing up from the top portion of the wall which separated the living area from the latrine. I grabbed a fire extinguisher and opened the latrine door. All I could see were flames and smoke. The fire extinguisher did little to stop the fire so I ran out into the Jamesway, which connected the five barracks buildings, in my long johns, cotton socks and Japanese slippers. Someone tried to use the local fire hydrant but it was frozen.

Staff Sergeant James Vreedenberg, from Operations, knew how to operate a CAT but the only one available was red-lined for repairs. Somehow he got it started and knocked down the Jamesway, which kept the fire from spreading and burning down the whole site.

But the barracks we were in was totally destroyed and some 20 of us had to crowd into the other two airmen's barracks and the NCO barracks with the clothes we were wearing as our only possessions.

As near as anyone could determine, the fire started because the Japanese Civil Engineering workers, who were supposed to clean the stoves, couldn't get to the site because of the snowstorm. Soot accumulated inside the stovepipe in the latrine, ignited, and started the fire.

Meanwhile the snow kept right on falling and then the site started to run out of food. The train with our replenishment rations had made it to the Abashiri RTO but there was no way to get the food to our site from the town, because of all the snow.

Helicopters and an SA-16 from Chitose made their way through the snow and paradropped enough C-rations, parkas, canvass cots, fire extinguisher refills and other necessities to see us through the crisis.

Finally, on Sunday, March 17, more than a week after it started and with nearly 170 inches of new snow on the ground, the storm came to an end.

Those of us who were in the barracks that burned had to go to Chitose Air Base and file claims. I think I got back about $350 for my clothes, camera, and the $195 I had placed in my locker. I never did get to go on leave to Sapporo, Misawa and Tokyo. But a month later I made it to Chitose to re-enlist - - and while there, I also got married.

Etsuko (Ruth) and I met at a St. Patrick's Day party the day I arrived at Abashiri Air Station. Shortly thereafter we started dating and after a lot of red tape we were married, some 13 months later. We're still happily married after more than 47 years, and have two sons and four grandchildren.

Along with the snowstorm, the fire and getting married, another thing that remains vividly in my mind was an incident that happened one day while I was on duty in radar maintenance. Sergeant Vreedenberg called me into Operations and told me he was perplexed because they had just tracked something that went across the upper portion of their PPI (Plan Position Indicator), traveling from the northwest to the southeast – a course that covered 225 miles in 15 seconds! Then it disappeared off the edge of the scope.

I checked out the PPI with our test parameters. Everything worked fine. This information was forwarded to ADCC at Misawa, which promptly informed us that we had a malfunction in our equipment because "nothing could travel that fast."

Ten days later we were visited by a security officer from Misawa who interrogated everyone about what we had seen. When he departed, his final words were,

"Remember, what you see here stays here." Years later I came to the conclusion that what we had tracked was a Russian missile that had gone awry and never achieved cruising altitude.

I was originally from St. Petersburg, Florida, and was in the Navy Reserves before I joined the Air Force in 1955 because I got tired of being seasick. I stayed in the Air Force after Abashiri and retired in October 1978, while stationed at Homestead AFB, Florida, with 26 years of military service.

Then I went to work with Honeywell Information Systems in Miami as a computer field engineer and also taught electronics in the Dade County Public School system for 18 years. That's why I was living in the Cutler Ridge area, south of Miami, when Hurricane Andrew struck on August 24, 1992. The storm tore off four trusses, 21 sheets of 4 x 8-foot plywood, and pushed out all the windows, but our house was left standing, although heavily damaged by the wind-driven saltwater and rain.

After retiring from the school system and to avoid any further disasters, we moved to Lake City, in north central Florida, on October 1,1996. Incredibly, four days after getting there, Hurricane Josephine barged in from the Gulf of Mexico. Fortunately, by the time it got to Lake City it had been downgraded to a tropical storm and damage was minimal.

Now we're content to take life a little easier and enjoy our family.

Frederick A. (Fred) Young, RR 2, Box 40270,
Lake City, FL 32024-7435. Phone 386/758-8850
e-mail:flyboy34@highstream.net

15

SURVIVING THE ELEMENTS AT A RADIO RELAY SITE

George (Mac) McCombs
Ground Radio Maintenance
Radio Relay Site 11 and Site 28, Abashiri
848th AC&W Squadron

The worst part about being at Relay 11, the isolated radio relay site which served Abashiri, Nemuro and the emergency landing strip at Kennebetsu, wasn't the boredom. There was always too much to do for that, maintaining the power units and the radio relay equipment.

The worst part was the weather – the snow and wind and cold – which affected everything we did. One time our thermometer showed a reading of 26 below zero. There were still patches of snow on the ground in June. And the winds were so strong they would suck the heat right out of the chimney of our oil stove, making it feel nearly as cold inside where we were as it was outside.

The site was perched atop a 2,650-foot high mountain which was an extinct volcano. Lake Mashu was located in the volcano crater. The relay was located about 67 miles south of Site 28 at Abashiri. The town of Teshikaga and civilization were seven miles away. For four and one-half miles out of town there was a dirt road. For the last two and one-half miles up the side of the mountain you just followed the ruts in the snow.

Usually you made it all the way up or down in one try. Sometimes you didn't. One time I threw a track on the weasel and could not see to put it back on in the dark. I dug a hole in a snow bank next to the weasel so that it was blocking the wind. I then crawled into the hole, curled up in my parka and spent a not too uncomfortable night until there was sufficient light to pry the track back on the weasel.

Another night I was driving a Japanese visitor up the mountain. We were just creeping along and I decided to have some fun. I pulled out the hand throttle, turned on the red dash lights, took my hands off the steering wheel and just let the front wheels follow the ruts.

"What are you doing?" my passenger stammered in a frightened voice as he peered first at the glowing lights on the instrument panel and then at the abandoned steering wheel.

"Oh, I'm just testing the new radar system on the truck," I explained with a straight face. I didn't think much more about it until several hours after we'd reached the top and Sato, one of the Japanese who helped us out at the site, got me aside and asked me what kind of crap I'd been feeding the passenger.

Jim Styers, who had been at the relay for around two years, was due to rotate to the states in September 1954. They told me I would replace him. Having been in the country for a total of two and a half months, my ability to speak Japanese was limited to about three words. So, Bill Shaffer, a radio operator, was sent with me to see that I got acclimated to the language and customs. Bill rotated to the states in December 1954 or January 1955. I remained the only American there until June 1955. Also at the site were five Japanese civilians who lived in Teshikaga. They had a rotating shift that would have them on the mountain for three days at a time. When I left Relay 11, JASDF personnel were phasing in with the ultimate goal of replacing the civilians.

Bill spoke some Japanese and that helped a lot on our frequent trips into Teshikaga. For food, we had C rations but we had no water for drinking or cooking. We had to go to town and fill five-gallon cans for that. While we were there we'd also buy eggs and onions to dress up the C rations. We used the public bathhouse for bathing.

Bill and I rented a hotel room in town in order to have a better and cleaner place to bathe. The room cost us $15 a month and the mama-san who owned the hotel treated us like long lost sons. She was always delighted for one or both of us to be in the bath when there were young female tourists using it as well. They were not accustomed to seeing Americans in a bathhouse and became very shy and embarrassed. Mama-san would tell them not to worry and introduce us as her sons, and say we were half-Japanese.

There were natural hot springs in and around Teshikaga. All the hotels, and I assume the private homes as well, used this very hot water in their baths. I could never figure out how they did it, but they could dig a well and get hot water, if that is what they wanted, or do the same and get cold water.

Fuel was critical to our operation. Without it we could not run our power units for electricity nor heat the building. Once a year, in the fall before it snowed, we would haul fuel up the hill. We would get a two and a half ton truck from Abashiri and a couple of extra troops to help load and unload. The fuel, gasoline and diesel, would arrive by rail in Teshikaga. We would get two boxcars loaded with 55-gallon drums. It took a couple of days to get them to the top of the hill. If my memory serves me right, we could get 23 drums per load on the truck. After unloading the drums at the relay site we would fill the truck with empty drums from the previous year and take them to the railhead to be loaded on the same two boxcars for return.

One time the tailgate on the truck broke and 23 of the 55-gallon drums rolled out and disappeared. Some we found later down the side of the mountain. Others were never found and presumably had tumbled into the lake, 1,500 feet below.

Abashiri and Relay 11 were my first real duty assignments in the Air Force. I arrived at Abashiri in July 1954 along with Nick Mattina and Harold Rosenberg. We were rumpled from the long train ride and wanted to look good before reporting to the site so we went in the public toilet in the RTO to change clothes and freshen up.

A short time later a driver from the site showed up with a Jeep and a quarter-ton trailer. He told us to throw our gear in the trailer, which was covered with two inches of mud. He said not to worry. It wouldn't make any difference by the time we got to the site.

He was right. Along the way, the Jeep bogged down in the mud and we all had to get out and push. When we got to the site we were covered in mud. Captain Allan Livers spotted us before we could check into the Orderly Room. "I was about to give the three of you an indoctrination speech," he laughed, "but I can see you've already been indoctrinated."

I was born and grew up in McKees Rocks, Pennsylvania, near Pittsburgh. I enlisted in the Air Force in May 1953 and attended ground radio maintenance school at Scott Air Force Base in Illinois. After my tour at Abashiri and Relay 11, I decided to stay in the Air Force and retired after 20 years and 10 days -- with all my time as a radio maintenance technician. With time, and increased rank and responsibilities, I had the opportunity to work on radar, teletype, crypto and computer equipment in addition to the radios. I also spent a couple of years at the Air Force satellite test facility in Sunnyvale, California, as a payload data analyst.

My second career was with E. I. duPont in Wilmington, Delaware. I started as a technician in photo products; spent several years in the distribution of consumables used with duPont automatic clinical analyzers, then went back into photo products. When I took early retirement at the age of 58 I was supervisor of 62 technicians.

Gertrude, my wife of more than 45 years, is from Smyrna, Delaware, so we stayed in the area. I bought an old jeep and became a rural mail carrier. Repairing the jeep, I found,was much more fun than delivering the mail. I also joined a service organization called the Ruritan Club. For fund raising purposes, we make sausage one night a month, October through April, and grind out up to 2,600 pounds in one evening. The proceeds from what we sell are used for community projects.

One of our sons is also in the Air Force at Hurlburt Field near Fort Walton Beach, Florida, where he's chief of vertical lift requirements for Air Force Special Operations. Another son teaches aircraft mechanics in San Antonio and we have a daughter who lives in Dubai, where her husband is a veterinary surgeon.

George M. (Mac)McCombs, 2379 Shaws Corner Road,
Clayton, DE 19938-3225. Phone 302/653-9410.
e-mail: geomac12@comcast.net

16

OKUSHIRI SHIMA –
THE ISLAND RADAR SITE

Nicholas (Nick) Gualillo
Radar Maintenance/Ground Power
Site 29, Okushiri Shima
848th AC&W Squadron

The first GIs who commissioned Site 29 arrived by LST, landing right on the beach. They brought with them the SCR 270 radar as well as everything else needed to establish a fully operational radar site.

The site was located atop Mount Kamui, at 1,918 feet the highest point on the island of Okushiri, some 20 miles west of Hokkaido in the Sea of Japan. The mountaintop had never been inhabited and was quite remote. The village of Okushiri was six miles away by a winding, muddy mountain road that was at times accessible only by a bulldozer ably driven by our J/N catskinner, named Takahashi.

The site was built by Japanese laborers, a number of whom were convicts or ex-convicts. The work was directed by a Mr.Ward, the contractor superintendent who lived in Otaru on Hokkaido with his Japanese wife. The first living quarters and the supply warehouse were Quonset huts. The combination mess hall, dayroom, bar and orderly room was made of something that looked like pressboard. Other buildings were frame with tile roofs.

Our main J/N KP and bartender was nicknamed Chibi, for Tiny, and he always had a smiling face and a friendly attitude. Another KP was believed to be a Communist spy and he was summarily fired.

The first site commander was Capt.Arthur Jehli. He was followed by Capt. Orville Brothers and then by Capt. Norman Walters, who was known for making some unauthorized low level passes over the site in his B-26, just to cheer up the troops.

The site was also buzzed by enemy MIGs a number of times. The 50-caliber machine guns and a Browning automatic rifle were broken out and we shot some trees down (to get a better view), but we never did get to shoot at the MIGs.

We also had a Philco tech rep named McLain who became somewhat of a hero by coming up with an idea to clear the frequently clogged commodes. He stuck a CO_2 fire extinguisher down the hole and blasted away. It worked well, so well, in fact, that he submitted the idea to 511th headquarters. His idea not only was turned down but he also got into fairly serious trouble for misuse of safety equipment. What the hell, it worked and continued to be surreptiously used when needed. I mean this was a quality of life issue -- a term unheard of in those days.

The island was supplied once or twice a month (weather permitting) by AKL 29, an MSTS vessel operating out of Otaru. It had two American civilians and a small crew of J/Ns. The American captain and the chief engineer always seemed pissed off at the world. The trip took at least 12 hours and the GIs were confined to a steel box, called a dog house, which was lashed to the deck. It was not a lot of fun.

A more pleasant but somewhat more roundabout way to reach the island was to go to Hakodate, spend the night there, take a train to Esashi and then take a ferry (read that fishing boat) to Okushiri. That way you were only on the water for about four hours. As I recall, we got RTO vouchers from Chitose to Esashi but we had to pay our own non-reimbursed costs for staying in Hakodate and taking the Japanese fishing boat to the island. To some of us it was worth it to avoid having to hang around Chitose or Otaru, waiting for the AKL. And besides, Hakodate was a great party town with very few GIs to compete with.

Either way you could tell you were getting close to the island by the intense smell, about five to ten miles off shore. It was an incredible stink in the summertime -- the odor of millions of drying squid. I still remember it. It's funny, though, once you were on the island for a while, you got used to it and didn't seem to mind it.

I was there from June 1952 through the early spring of 1953 and I had a great time. I roamed all over the island, just me and my shotgun, blasting at crows, getting trapped in some ravines I almost never got out of, visiting the other side of the island where no GI had ever been and finding very friendly people who had virtually nothing but were more than willing to share a watermelon or a cup of tea with a foreigner.

One time I got lost and ended up in the Communist off-limits town of Aonae and had to hike back 13 miles along the coast road to Okushiri town. There I contacted the site CO through the Japanese police to let him know I was only lost -- and not AWOL.

While at Okushiri Shima I never did much in radar maintenance since my training had been as an airborne radar mechanic, although I managed to put in quite a few nights as a "scope dope" on the Rock. After Site 29, I spent 90 days at Hiroshima attending an Army specialist school in heavy equipment. Then I was assigned to Site 18 at Wakkanai, where I worked in the Motor Pool (until I froze my feet), and then went on TDY to the Motor Pool at Site 36 at Erimo Zaki, since they didn't have any trucks running. Finally I was sent to Misawa and assigned to the 49th Motor Vehicle Squadron Ground Power Repair Shop and then was reassigned to the 511th radar site powerhouse at Hilltop.

While I was still at Okushiri Shima I had to have my tonsils removed and was sent to the base hospital at Misawa. During my recovery, one of the nurses would bring me ice cream. Her name was Hisako and we were married in August 1954 at the U.S. Consulate in Sapporo after fighting the military authorities who were under orders to discourage all military marriages to Japanese Nationals.

I stayed in the Air Force after my first experience in Japan and we returned for another tour of duty in the Tokyo area from 1965 to 1969. Then, in 2002, we returned to Japan again, this time on vacation and, while my wife visited family and friends on Northern Honshu, I returned to Okushiri Shima -- 49 years after I had said goodbye.

The changes are incredible and most of them have occurred since July 12, 1993, when an earthquake measuring 7.8 on the Richter Scale and a tsunami towering 30 feet devastated the island, killing more than 230 people and leaving hundreds of others homeless. Today there are few signs of the disaster.

A paved road now circles almost the entire island and rental cars are available. I never did get all the way up to our old camp at the top of Mount Kamui because the Japanese Air Force has posted no trespassing signs on the access road. Even more disappointing was the fact that the site was in the clouds during the time I was there and I never could see it or take pictures.

Tourism and sport fishing are growing industries and the island has become a favorite weekend destination for summertime tourists from Sapporo. Two large and comfortable ferry boats service Okushiri (no more being cooped up in a "doghouse" on deck) and Twin Otters fly a regular schedule into Aonae on the south end of the island, which has the only land flat enough for an airfield.

I spent a night at the Midori-Kan, an onsen (hot spring) resort that none of us in the 1950s could ever have imagined being built in such a primitive and inaccessible place. To say it was beautiful would be an understatement. My room had twin beds, satellite TV, a writing desk, a sparkling clean Western style bathroom, and a great mountain view. The food, both Japanese and Western style, was delicious. And best of all was the bill: 11,100 yen, or about $95, including the meals. I still don't know why it was so low but I was assured it was correct.

An even more pleasant surprise was to discover that the island no longer reeks with the odor from the squid drying racks, which used to greet us miles from shore. Squid is still a major catch but apparently it now is processed in a different manner.

As a general observation, Japan today is a country of great variation, from its very visible modernization to the not so visible traditional, which is still very important in the day-to-day life of most Japanese.

The girls seem better looking than ever and the people, male and female, seem noticeably taller than they were 50 years ago. Coloring the hair is a big fad. Red and brunette are especially popular with the girls. Many younger men color their hair red or blond, which I thought looked pretty weird.

Very good toll roads, complete with modern rest stops, now connect all major parts of the country, but the tolls are very high. Modern gas stations and convenience stores are everywhere, with names like KFC, MacDonald's, Mr. Coffee and 7-Eleven. Virtually every teenager has a cell phone stuck in their ear as do many businessmen and average people.

In short, Japan is a beautiful country, full of contrasts which we as Westerners will probably never understand. And it is expensive almost beyond comprehension. How the average worker copes with day-to-day expenses is a mystery to me.

Nick Gualillo died on October 15, 2004 while he and his wife were on a return visit to Northern Japan. He was a resident of Ruskin, Florida, near Tampa, and was an ardent participant in activities of the 511th Reunion Association.

17

FINDING THE SECURITY FENCE 12 FEET STRAIGHT DOWN

Richard F. (Dick) Loose
Commander, Site 18, Wakkanai
848th AC&W Squadron

Site 18 at Wakkanai became operational in 1949 so it was still pretty new when I became site commander in 1951.

Our primary mission, of course, was to keep an eye out for enemy aircraft and that wasn't hard to do considering our location. It was 30 miles across the strait from the northern tip of Hokkaido, where we were, to the southern tip of the Sakhalin Islands, which were placed under Russian control at the end of World War II. The MacArthur Line, which divided us, was halfway between, or just 15 miles away, and from Radar Hill we could clearly see Russian-held territory.

We'd track their aircraft as they came off the ground and gain altitude until they would start flying a racetrack pattern alongside the MacArthur line. We'd notify ADCC at Misawa and they'd scramble F-84s to fly up and keep the MIGs company and dare each other to cross the line.

We also had to track our own B-29s and B-50s on reconnaissance flights from bases farther south in Japan. And sometimes we would track an aging C-47 which was loaded with ECM (electronic countermeasure) equipment and flew out of Misawa to test the effectiveness of our radar sites on Hokkaido at overcoming the jamming strategies of the Russians.

Unfortunately these reconnaissance flights always took place at night and I would always have to stay up in case anything unusual happened, which it sometimes did.

One B-29 pilot got a little confused -- or perhaps a little over-enthused -- and flew across the line. A couple of MIGs jumped him and he did a 180 and made it back across the line safely, whereupon he turned around and did the same thing a second time. This time the MIGs got their message across and the last we saw of him on our radar he was hightailing it due south. A year or two later another B-29 on a similar mission near Nemuro in eastern Hokkaido wasn't so fortunate. But, as we say in Texas, that's a whole other story.

If tracking aircraft was all we had to do, being the site commander would have been a pretty good job. But, as I learned, reconnaissance flights were not the only things higher headquarters sent us from down south.

One day I had to meet a colonel who was arriving on some sort of an inspection visit. He took an instant dislike to me, to the site and to the weather, which felt like it was 30 below (probably because it was).

I took him on a little tour and he demanded to know where our security fence was. I suggested that he get a shovel and start digging and he'd find the fence 12 feet down. He didn't think that was funny and accused me of being insubordinate. A couple of weeks later I heard through the grapevine that I was going to be court-martialed. I thought that sounded like a pretty good deal since it would get me out of the cold and let me thaw out for a while in Tokyo.

But before anything happened, Major James Shelly, the 511th adjutant, called and asked if I had really told the colonel to get a shovel and start digging. I told him I had and he said he thought that was one of the funniest things he had ever heard. He said that when the general at JADF heard about it he also thought it was funny and the charges were going to be dropped. So I didn't get the trip to Tokyo.

The troops at the site seemed to take a certain amount of pride in being ornery and I guess I felt the same way. I mean, what was someone going to do if we screwed up? Send us to an isolated radar site?

When I arrived at Wakkanai we had about 40 troops and when I left in August 1953 we had about 100. I tried to convince them that if we were going to survive comfortably we'd have to do it ourselves. So everyone pitched in and built a bar that rivaled the ones in many of the posh clubs in more habitable areas of Japan.

The weather, of course, was impossible. Snow. Wind. Cold. All at the same time.

One time the wind blew the snow over the road to Radar Hill and it was so deep that we had to hire 30 Japanese women for 15 days to dig a tunnel for us to get a weasel through the drifts. We paid them each a dollar a day and let them have our leftover food.

I wasn't trained for things like that when I got my wings and was commissioned a second lieutenant in February 1949. But you did what you had to do.

Originally, I had enlisted in the old Army Air Corps right after Pearl Harbor. I figured the beans would be better in the Army than at home in Newton, Kansas. I got out of the service when the war ended, then went back in as an aviation cadet in 1948.

When my tour at Wakkanai was over I left active duty and attended Oklahoma A&M for three years while serving in the Air Force Reserve. In March 1957 I was recalled to active duty and finally retired as a major in 1967.

I went to work for Electro-Systems, a divison of Ling Temco Vought, as a quality engineer for C-130 gunship electronics. Then I joined Texas Instruments and worked in configuration management until I retired in 1980. We lived in western Colorado for several years, then moved back to Texas in 1986. My wife, Margaret, bought a small business in Tyler in 1989 and we live in Van, which is about 25 miles away.

Dick Loose, P.O. Box 1351, Van, TX. 75790-1351.
Phone 903/963-7642. e-mail: thelooses@webtv.net

18

'YOU GUYS PROBABLY JUST PICKED UP MARS'

Gene R. Couch
Radar Operator, Site 45, Ishikari Tobetsu
848th AC& W Squadron

When I arrived at Site 45 in 1957, the NCO barracks was full so I lived with the troops for two months.

One night there was a card game going on near the foot of my bed and one of the guys became enraged and started screaming at another player, "You SOB. I saw what you did. You cheated the pot out of a nickel."

None of the other players could calm the guy down and finally he jumped up and stalked away. Suddenly he reappeared with a carbine and before anyone could stop him he pointed it point blank at the player he accused of cheating and pulled the trigger.

There was a loud "CLICK."

With that, six of us leaped on the guy with the gun and wrestled him to the floor. Just then, the provost sergeant came rushing into the barracks, saw what was going on, grabbed the carbine, pulled the trigger – and blew a hole in the ceiling.

For what seemed like an eternity, there was dead silence. The airman who'd been the target was as white as you could get. Then he asked the provost sergeant, "Can I have the empty casing?"

He had a necklace made and wore the empty casing as a reminder of what had happened. His accuser was taken to Chitose and put behind bars. Every time the guy he tried to kill had a chance, he'd go to Chitose to visit his attacker and take him cigarettes. "When he pointed that gun at me and pulled the trigger," he explained, "I saw the light. I started reading the Bible and decided the only right thing to do was forgive him and try to be his friend."

I had been in the Air Force for well over three years and was a staff sergeant when I got to the site in February. My primary assignment after finishing radar school at Keesler and being assigned to Japan was with the 738th AC&W Squadron at Olathe Naval Air Station in Kansas, where we worked on developing better systems for tracking aircraft and passing the control of in-flight planes from one location to another. Some of the things we worked on have been modified and are still being used by the FAA today.

It's too bad we didn't have some of that technology at Site 45 the time we spotted a strange object in the sky for three straight nights. When viewed from outside, the object was about the size of a silver dollar held at arm's length. It was circular and was a brilliant white except for the lower third, which looked as if it had five reddish-bluish flames shooting out of it – about the color of a blow torch – with two of the flames on one side and three on the other.

The object did not appear on our search radar but did show up on our height finder. Each night we scrambled fighters out of Chitose and then the object would disappear straight up – from 4,000 feet on the height finder to over 40,000 feet. We dutifully reported all of this to the authorities down south, who told us, "You guys probably just picked up Mars."

But we had also taken five rolls of film, shot at a variety of exposures, which we developed in our site photo lab. Would you believe every roll turned out to be overexposed? So we never did find out what we saw.

Altogether, I spent 26 years and 10 days in the Air Force, much of it involved in more advanced, computerized systems for aircraft control and some of it in the "Human Reliability Program," which was a highly classified system for nuclear control. But the memories of Site 45 are still clear in my mind. Like the little owl that flew through an open door into our operations room and became our mascot. We named him Fubar – for "Fouled Up Beyond All Recognition" – and he became so tame we fed him by hand. He was still there when I left and maybe he's still there, living off the Japanese Air Defense Force.

My last duty station before retiring was in Germany, which is where I met my current wife, Ruthann. She was also in the Air Force, as an air weapons controller. We were married in Switzerland in 1978.

When I retired at McGuire AFB in New Jersey in 1979 she was separated from active duty at the same time. A few months later we bought a motor home and a small car to tow behind it and for the next two and one-half months we toured the U.S. until we reached my hometown of Eugene, Oregon. It was one of the best trips I ever made.

In 1981, the FAA hired Ruthann as a controller in San Francisco. As she climbed the ranks in the FAA over the next 24 years I followed her. We lived in Palo Alto, California; Seattle, and Salt Lake City before she landed the FAA manager's job at the Eugene airport in 1997. I ask you, what are the odds of your wife being assigned to your own hometown?

When someone asks me what I do (besides follow Ruthann), I tell them I'm just a bum. If I really want to dazzle them, I tell them I'm a "Landlord of Multiple Housing," which means I'm involved in buying, refurbishing, managing, renting and selling rental properties. Right now, we have seven properties in Eugene and one in New Jersey (near Ruthann's brother, who's in real estate). We also have other properties in Arizona and Colorado but have sold the ones we had in California.

Much of the rest of our time is spent with our son and three grandsons.

Gene R. Couch, 3250 Whitbeck Blvd., Eugene, OR 97405-5108. Phone 541/334-5108.
e-mail:couchruthanngene@qwest.net

19

'GO HOME, YANKEE DOG'

Bob Misrach
Aircaft Controller, Site 28, Abashiri
848th AC&W Squadron

The jukebox was already sitting on the steps outside the officers' club at Misawa Air Base when the Club Officer discovered what was happening and rushed to the scene.

Before the Club Officer could say a word, one of the three officers manhandling the jukebox stuck out his hand and the unsuspecting officer grabbed it. "Hi, meat," the second lieutenant said. "I'm Bob Misrach. Lock this joint up for the night and come on over to my room. We've got some Japanese women there and we'll really have a blast. We need the jukebox for music."

About noon the next day the jukebox still blared in Misrach's BOQ room. The Club Officer and assorted other officers and women were strewn about the tiny room in various stages of drunken repose.

Misrach himself was two miles out in the flatlands off the edge of the base, guzzling coffee as he stared at a radar screen and vectored aircraft through the sky with all of the mastery that comes with being a new graduate from

Aircraft Controller's School. The knot on his tie hung down to the middle of his shirt. His blue uniform was splattered with beer. And when he wasn't droning "Roger" into a microphone he was telling all who would listen, "Come on over tonight and we'll *really* have a party."

Bob Misrach (never Second Lieutenant Misrach) had arrived in Northern Japan. Within two weeks the commander of the 511th Aircraft Control & Warning Group had tired of Misrach's antics and ordered him sent northward to an isolated radar site perched atop a mountain, 10 miles from the fishing village of Abashiri, on Japan's northernmost island of Hokkaido.

When Misrach left Hokkaido 18 months later, his name may have been the most famous (or infamous) on Hokkaido. If it wasn't, it was not because of any lack of effort on his part. And his renown was not limited to northern Japan.

Lieutenant Colonel Nolan C. Hatcher, commander of the 848th Aircraft Control & Warning Squadron on Hokkaido, recalled how he made a visit to Fifth Air Force Headquarters in Nagoya in south central Japan and struck up a conversation with a major in the officers' club. The major wanted to know where Colonel Hatcher was stationed and what he did and then astounded Colonel Hatcher by saying that he had, indeed, heard of the 848th AC&W Squadron.

"Don't you have a lieutenant up there by the name of Misrach, who's always stirring up some sort of trouble?" he asked.

With that, one of the Japanese waitresses interrupted. "Lieutenant Misrach?" she asked. "Skoshi (little) lieutenant?

Always talk and call everbody meat-san? He come here maybe two weeks ago. Go out with Janie-san. She get stinko."

Everyone thought Misrach was from San Francisco but the truth is he was born in War, West Virginia. But he did grow up in San Francisco and somehow he managed to obtain an ROTC commission in the Air Force when he graduated from the University of California. Then came Japan and Abashiri.

When he arrived at the site in the fall of 1954, he immediately took it upon himself to improve morale for the 85 enlisted men and officers. One of his first self-appointed assignments was to procure floor lamps and lampshades for the day room. Six times he typed out requisitions, signed his name and sent the forms directly to higher authority at Misawa for approval. And six times the requisitions bounced because Misrach had not forwarded them through proper channels.

So Misrach wrote to Macy's in New York City and ordered a dozen floor lamps and shades and charged the order to Special Services at Misawa. Within six weeks the shipment had traveled 9,000 miles to Abashiri. And the paperwork went to Misawa, where it reportedly took 10 months to decide whether the order should be returned or the bill should be paid (which turned out to be the final decision).

Then there was the day a new maid came to work at Site 28 and Misrach decided she should be taught the English language. Day after day, Misrach would closet himself in his room with the maid, presumably teaching her English behind the closed door.

The fruits of his labor were realized one night when Colonel Hatcher visited the site. After dinner, Colonel Hatcher and the detachment's handful of officers gathered around the tiny bar for a friendly chat. All except Misrach, who was conspicuous by his absence.

Suddenly a door opened and Fuji-san hesitantly entered the room and approached Colonel Hatcher. "Fuji-san speak English," she giggled. "You listen?"

"Very nice. Of course," said Colonel Hatcher, who was always interested in bettering relations with the Japanese. "What can you say?"

"Remember Pearl Harbor," Fuji-san squealed. "Go home, Yankee dog."

Misrach's most notable accomplishment was wangling a deal to take USO shows to the radar sites. Before Misrach, the shows had toured radar sites in Greenland, Alaska and other far flung points. But their visits to Japan had always been confined to the major bases.

Through his connections with friends in the states, Misrach changed all of that. There were only two tours, but personnel at the radar detachments, who hadn't seen a "round-eye" in a year or two, thought they were the greatest.

By cargo plane, third class train, converted Navy LST's and jeeps, the troupes each played at 12 remote early warning sites from Tokyo northward, conquering rolling winter seas to get to island detachments and battling foot-deep mud and 30-foot snow drifts as they climbed mountains to others.

Misrach, of course, was master of ceremonies and the shows were never dull. In the middle of one act, Misrach would snuggle up to a bosomy accordion player and motion for her to stop playing. Then he'd move the accordion a few inches away from her amply endowed breasts. "Be careful," he'd whisper loudly. "These troops haven't seen anything like you in a long time. They don't want any accidents."

Ultimately, and somewhat against his will, Misrach was promoted to first lieutenant, which prompted Colonel Hatcher to comment, "He's the sorriest aircraft controller I've ever seen and also the worst officer. But he's put the 848th on the map."

Misrach's departure from Japan was even more conspicuous than his arrival. For a long time Misrach had the idea that when his tour of duty in Japan was up, he wanted to return home "in the other direction" and see the rest of the world, rather than returning to California as U.S. military personnel always did.

To pull this off, Misrach needed a stroke of luck and he got it when Duane Traylor, another officer at Abashiri, severely mashed his forefinger in a Jeep accident . Traylor, who was from Wichita, Kansas, was sent to a hospital in Tokyo. While he was recovering he spent several hours with two master sergeants in the FEAF personnel section who showed him an obscure FEAF regulation which authorized U.S. Air Force personnel to be separated from active duty in Japan.

Misrach was elated when Traylor gave him the news. He immediately convinced Traylor and a third officer at Abashiri, Pat Wise of Vancluse, South Carolina, that they should be separated from active duty in Tokyo and return to the U.S. by a leisurely tour of Hong Kong, Singapore, India, the Middle East, Europe and other stops along the way.

Complying with the FEAF regulation and obtaining all of the necessary approvals proved to be a major exercise and for more than two months the red tape piled up. One of the Catch-22 problems was that the State Department refused to issue a passport to military personnel -- but the Air Force said that no one could be discharged or separated from active duty while still in Japan unless they *had* a passport.

The three needed statements from their commander, their commander's commander, a letter from the American Embassy (regarding the passport), a letter from the Japanese Immigration Department, and even an offer of employment from a Japanese businessman. Colonel Hatcher, perhaps not altogether unhappy over Misrach's impending departure, proved of great assistance and in a flurry of last minute excitement that included getting the personal approval of FEAF Major General Roger Ramey, the three set sail from Kobe on January 24, 1956.

Six months later the journey concluded in New York City. Traylor and Wise went home. And Misrach returned to San Francisco and reportedly went into real estate sales. Efforts to locate him in more recent years have been unsuccessful. One account said that he lived in Australia for a year and then spent a year in Israel before returning to San Francisco.

But he's still remembered by those he made laugh with his antics on Hokkaido.

The preceding account was based largely on information written about Misrach in the 1950s, while he was still stationed at Abashiri. It was reviewed for accuracy in 2002 by Pat Wise, who was one of Misrach's traveling companions on the journey home. Pat can be reached at 1204 Plantation Drive, Simpsonville, SC 29681-4723. Phone: 864/962-869. e-mail: pwise14202@aol.com

20

LIFE IN THE 848TH

Traveling, Living and Working
Beyond the End of the Line

> *The report which follows is based on a 1954 study of conditions faced by personnel of the 511th AC&W Group assigned to radar sites of the 848th AC&W Squadron on Hokkaido. The name of the author was not included with the report on file at the Air Force Historical Research Agency at Maxwell Air Force Base.*

One of the biggest problems facing all of the radar sites on Hokkaido is transportation -- getting supplies, personnel and food to their point of use. All of the sites are isolated and depend on long, varied and often hazardous means of transportation.

The backbone of the transportation network is the Japanese National Railway system which fans out from Chitose Air Base to the station nearest each site. The trains, unless delayed by heavy snowfall, run on time and are generally efficient. The problems occur between the point where the rail line ends and the sites themselves. The distances vary but all are long enough to present problems. The detachment at Erimo-Zaki (Site 36) is 27 miles from the railroad's terminus; at Shikotsu (Site 45) the distance is seven miles. The rail line serving Okushiri-Shima (Site 29), an island off the southwest coast of Hokkaido, ends at Otaru. From there it's a 12 to 20-hour trip over water (depending on the weather), plus an additional eight-mile trip by road from the dock to the detachment.

Regardless of the distances, it is often impossible to travel the final miles to the sites. When this occurs, the sites are shut off from the outside world.

There are three reasons for the transportation problem: The weather, the lack of proper vehicles and equipment, and the roads themselves. During the winter there is almost constant snowfall and, even with daily snow removal efforts, a sudden windstorm or blizzard can create impassable drifts, completely blocking the roads.

Snow removal equipment at the sites is limited to one D-8 and one D-6 Caterpillar tractor, both inadequate for snow removal during a Hokkaido winter. Due to the shortage of parts and the heavy workload, the tractors are frequently out of service for repair. When they are in running condition, even they can become trapped in the snow. One slid into a ditch at one site and it was necessary to chain logs to the tracks for added traction.

The narrowness of the road to Erimo-Zaki caused an Air Force truck to slide off and turn over, seriously injuring an airman. At many other sites, vehicles have also slipped off the roads and sometimes been totally buried by the snow.

The M-29 cargo carriers provided to each of the sites for snow travel are almost worthless. The vehicles are so old (most were built in 1942) that parts are worn beyond repair and replacement parts are extremely scarce. Also, the detachments do not have the personnel or the equipment to perform a major overhaul on these vehicles. The result is that none, or perhaps only one, may be in operating condition at any given time. The vehicles carry only three passengers and are not at all satisfactory as a primary means of winter transportation.

Improved roads plus better snow removal equipment would enable wheel-driven vehicles to be used throughout the year. This would simplify the problem of keeping the logistical lifelines open.

Transportation within the sites is also a major problem during the winter. The huge amounts of snow frequently isolate DF stations. Personnel have often had to exist on whatever C-rations were in the buildings when they became snowed in because the on-site snow-removal equipment could not clear the roads.

After one particularly heavy snowstorm at Wakkanai (Site 18), the DF station was isolated without food for 32 hours. It took a detail of 50 men a full day to clear enough snow for a tractor-mounted Weasel to get through.

Most radar operations buildings are located on mountaintops some distance from their base camps. The roads are usually very steep and narrow, and are easily made impassable by the snow. Until a tractor can clear enough snow for a Weasel to get through, shift change personnel must clear their own path, often taking two or three hours to make their way through the snow on foot.

Summer and the melting snow present problems of their own. This is especially true at Okushiri-Shima (Site 29), where the heavy spring and summer rains combine with the melting snow to obscure the roads in a sea of mud.

Millions of dollars have been spent equipping the sites with the latest in electronic equipment. But the investment is imperiled by the transportation problems. No matter how much equipment and food is available for the radar sites, it is of little value if it does not reach its destination when needed.

Living conditions at the radar sites -- the quarters, recreational facilities, chapels, and laundry and dry cleaning facilities -- vary in quantity and quality, but generally are poor. Morale, which is always a concern because of the isolated location of the sites, becomes an even greater concern when the living conditions are substandard.

Many of the quarters, although they cannot be compared to the comfortable facilities being constructed at some bases in Japan, at least provide the essentials of a sheltered place to sleep. Many other quarters however are overcrowded, have few if any lockers or furniture, and do not have the space for these amenities even if they did exist. The average space per man at Okushiri-Shima (Site 29) is 40 cubic feet, less than half that required by Air Force medical authorities.

The latrine facilities at both Okushiri-Shima and Wakkanai are so poor that 75 men at each site have to use one latrine, equipped with one commode, one shower and one wash basin. To make matters worse, the latrines are not connected to the various barracks, so it is necessary for the men to walk more than a block in most cases, often through heavy snowstorms and deep drifts, just to reach the facilities. At Okushiri-Shima only five or six men out of a total of 75 can take a shower on any given night because that is all the hot water that is available. And there is no heat in the latrines and temperatures often drop below zero.

The poor quality of construction makes many of the barracks cold and drafty in the winter and dusty in the summer. Roofs and windows often leak so badly that snow has to be shoveled from the floors after a storm.

At one radar site, the one room, six-cot Visiting Officers Quarters, which often is filled, can have four to six inches of snow on the floor. There are no lockers, chests of drawers or other facilities for clothing and luggage. There also are no latrine facilities in the building and the tent stove frequently shuts down when water freezes in the fuel line.

Recreational facilities at the detachments are also very limited. This takes on added importance since facilities in the nearest Japanese towns are also nonexistent in most cases.

The main problem is the lack of building space to house recreational equipment where the men can "let off steam." Some indoor recreation, such as ping-pong and pool tables, is available on a limited basis, and, of course, there is always card playing and other indoor games. But there is nowhere for the men to work out and engage in physical exercise. More often, the only place to go is the nearest bar.

If small buildings could be erected on each site, large enough for a boxing ring, weight lifting equipment and perhaps a half-sized basketball court, the situation would be greatly improved.

Another deficiency at the sites is the lack of facilities for religious services, a shortcoming magnified by the isolation of the sites and the long tour of duty away from family life. At one site, a chapel was built and furnished at no cost to the Air Force or the U.S. Government. Money, materials and labor all were donated by site personnel since detachments in the 511th AC&W Group are not authorized chapels.

Laundry facilities are in extremely poor condition and most detachments have no dry cleaning facilities, nor do nearby towns. The cleaning of blue uniforms and civilian clothes must be done during a TDY trip, or while on leave. What little laundry equipment does exist is old and almost impossible to repair. Replacement parts are virtually nonexistent.

At one site the water heater had to be made out of a POL drum and a tent stove. The 50-gallon capacity of the heater must supply the laundry water for nearly 150 men. The two clothes dryers at the same site were originally diesel-heated but the heating elements became so worn that clothes came out covered with diesel fuel. New units were not available, so site personnel built electrical units that, while very unsatisfactory, are the only method of drying clothes.

Working conditions at the sites are greatly hampered by the weather, the equipment, clothing and building facilities.

Each winter, Hokkaido receives an average of 140 inches of snow, with six feet remaining on the ground most of the time. The average high temperature in the winter is 27 degrees and the average low is one degree above zero. Winds at the radar sites are frequently between 25 and 40 knots. These are averages. At the radar sites, the snowfall is often much heavier, the temperatures much lower and the winds much higher, sometimes exceeding 100 knots. Snowfall has been so deep at some of the sites that trucks and entire buildings have been completely buried.

Because the buildings are not constructed for weather this severe, the snow has collapsed several of the structures and the wind has damaged many others. Tents are sometimes used in place of permanent storage and working facilities but they are even more susceptible to weather damage.

The hauling and storage of POL is greatly impeded by the snow. While it might seem advisable to deliver a full year's supply of POL to each site during the warmer months, the lack of storage facilities makes this impossible. Often during the winter, storage drums are buried by the snow and many of them remain lost until the summer thaw.

Heating systems for the work areas are frequently inadequate and sometimes nonexistent. Many "lash-up" type heating arrangements have been tried but most have proven inadequate and some are serious fire hazards.

Authorized clothing for outdoor work is similarly deficient and suffers in comparison with that provided to military personnel in Korea, Alaska and other areas where cold weather prevails. One of the most desperate needs is for heavy, Arctic type shoepacks, such as those authorized in Korea. The only footwear now provided is a pair of rubber overshoes.

Many other problems affect the working conditions at the radar sites, nearly all of them due to the simple fact that the building facilities and authorized equipment are not adequate for the harsh extremes of winter in Hokkaido.

21

Epilogue

The Best Is Yet
To Come

As was mentioned in the prologue, this is not intended to be the end of "Cold War in a Cold Place." An expanded second edition is already in the works.

Which leads me to one final thought on what this book is really all about. I no longer remember whether it was when we were gathered at the 511th reunion banquet in Nashville or Arlington or Branson, or in Charleston or somewhere else, and I no longer remember the name of the speaker, but I've never forgotten something he said. In essence it was this:

"I think you'll detect more love in this room right now, than you'll find in most churches on Sunday."

Jerry Hanks